To Heal As Jesus Healed

To Heal As Jesus Healed

Barbara Leahy Shlemon,
Dennis Linn, S.J. and
Matthew Linn, S.J.

AVE MARIA PRESS
Notre Dame, Indiana 46556

First printing, April, 1978
Third printing, September, 1979
62,000 copies in print

Imprimi Potest:

    Bruce F. Biever, S.J.
    Provincial

Library of Congress Catalog Card Number: 78-54126
International Standard Book Number: 0-87793-152-6

Cover photo by John David Arms.
Manufactured in the United States of America.

Contents

Introduction

Fathers Matt and Dennis Linn and I were giving a workshop at St. Vincent Hospital in Toledo, Ohio, when they first suggested I collaborate on writing a book. They showed me a preliminary outline, which greatly interested me because it involved exploring the new Roman Catholic rite for the Sacrament of the Sick.

In my first book, *Healing Prayer,*[1] I described the tremendous changes which occurred in my nursing career after observing a patient healed through sacramental anointing. The year was 1964 and the rite was then known as Extreme Unction, the "final anointing." In this case, however, it became not a preparation for death but a blessing which conferred physical healing and new life.

The new Rite of Anointing encourages the whole Church to recognize healing prayer as a normal factor in our Christian lives. We are told to expect that physical healing and wholeness will result from utilizing the power of the sacrament, and we are called to deepen our faith in God's willingness to make us healthy.

Unfortunately, there remains in the minds of

many a great deal of confusion surrounding the use of this sacrament. They continue to refer to it as the Last Rites, as the final anointing, to be given only as death is approaching. Some hospital patients who have not been instructed in the purpose of the new rite have become hysterical when the priest began to administer the Sacrament of the Sick, requiring sedation and hours of reassurance concerning their physical condition.

Others receive the anointing with very little faith in its ability to heal their illnesses. They view the sacrament as a nice ritual and a gesture of comfort by the Church, but they fail to appropriate the power for wholeness which it offers.

On the other hand, many Christians *are* appropriating the power for healing which they find available not only through the new rite of anointing, but also through prayers for physical healing. For example, in the summer of 1977, 800 priests attended a healing service in Steubenville, Ohio. Because of the powerful prayers of their fellow priests, by the end of that evening 500 priests had stood to claim a physical healing.

As I travel around the country teaching Christians to pray for their sick, I'm discovering a tremendous desire on the part of the laity to become channels for God's healing love. In my home parish, Light of Christ Catholic Church, Clearwater, Florida, a brief announcement was read one Sunday morning, inviting people to volunteer for an intercessory telephone prayer-chain. Without any further explanation, 88 individuals signed up to pray for others, especially for the physical healing of the sick. Such a response indicates a desire to answer some of the more common questions about healing prayer, such as:

what is God's will concerning suffering? who has the gifts to minister to the sick?

It is my hope that this book will dispel some of the confusion surrounding both the official Rite of Anointing and unofficial prayers for physical healing, thereby encouraging more of the faithful to receive the wholeness available through these methods. They are tremendous sources of grace and life, freely given to us by a heavenly Father who loves us more deeply than we can ask for or imagine.

—Barbara

Prologue
The Struggle to Pray for Physical Healing

I learned the hard way about stepping forward to pray with others for physical healing. Five years ago I gave a 30-day retreat to Carol, whose deafness made it necessary for her to lip-read. For 30 days we met for one hour each day. During this time I felt that, if I were to pray with her about her deafness, her hearing could be restored. But what if I prayed with Carol and her hearing wasn't restored? Her faith might be weakened, making it difficult during the retreat for Carol to trust God, let alone to trust her retreat director.

Day after day, as I directed Carol, I entertained many thoughts of praying with her for a restoration of her hearing. At times I would consider how miracles happened only in the early Church, when atheists needed the witness value of miracles. As those thoughts drifted by, I would thank God that our generation was beyond needing miracles of physical healing. I rationalized about how fortunate Carol and I were because her deafness could call both of us to greater faith.

Yet, on other days, I could convince myself that maybe God would heal small things like my upset stomach, but probably nothing as big as deafness. I remembered a few times when I did pray about "big" things such as cancer and not much change had taken place. In one instance, the person was inconsiderate enough to die on me—and I wasn't prepared to experience another "failure."

Because I feared failing and had lost confidence in Jesus working through my prayers, I started thinking of ways in which Carol might be healed. I could concede that Jesus might heal Carol's condition only if she went to a special place such as Lourdes or Fatima, or only if she had someone special like Kathryn Kuhlman pray with her. My 12 years of intellectual seminary training came in handy as I imagined ways that Jesus might heal Carol, ways which would not involve me.

For 30 days I struggled, trying to involve myself in facing Carol's deafness with her. In the end, my fears won out. I failed to discuss her condition, avoided praying with her about it, and she left the retreat as physically deaf as she came in.

Even though I had given up, Carol had not. A year later I received a letter from her telling me: "I can hear dripping water, people behind me, birds, wind. . . . it is all like music." She had asked some friends to pray over her and her hearing was totally restored! Jesus ignored all my tip-toeing around; he healed Carol without demanding that she find Kathryn Kuhlman or journey to Lourdes. Carol's physicians confirmed that her hearing was normal, despite the fact that she still has the same physical damage (genetic neural defect with auditory nerve damage). Four years have passed and Carol continues to hear normally—even while carrying on phone conversations with her chicken-hearted retreat director.

When I heard that a group of friends had prayed and Jesus had restored Carol's hearing, I felt both delighted and sad. I felt delighted that Carol could hear, but saddened that I hadn't stepped out to pray with her. I also felt saddened when I remembered the other people I had passed by and left to suffer, simply because I had neglected to pray for physical healing with them.

That sadness helped me to say "yes." "Yes, I will try to face problems with people like Carol and, when appropriate, offer to pray for physical healing." I was willing to begin putting to death my desire to be in control of every situation, and to allow Jesus to act his most loving way through me.

After I said "yes" to praying for physical healing, I was still left with the question of how to pray with someone like Carol. How do you pray for physical healing when, first of all, a person is willing to be prayed with and, second, when you sense that the time is right and you should be the one to do the praying?

In trying to discover healthy ways in which the Spirit might lead us to pray, Matt and I found ourselves drawn to ask Christians from many denominations to pray with us. No longer is healing prayer limited to the Pentecostal or Assembly of God Churches. Episcopalians (especially since the 1908 Lambeth Conference) and Roman Catholics (especially since the new Rite of Anointing in 1974), anoint their sick with oil and expect physical healing.

I received one of my greatest surprises in the use of anointing with oil when Matt and I attended a weekly healing service in an Episcopalian Church. This anointing service, filled with people on a Wednesday morning, celebrated two things. First, the physical healings that had occurred since last week's service and, second, the physical healings that they were currently seeking.

Since that Wednesday morning, we have witnessed the healing power of God in many Christian churches. Even in the few nonsacramental churches where there is no anointing with oil, much of their prayer for physical healing is based on traditional anointing rites, or on the same scriptural foundation.

Each of the following chapters will deal with one of the 12 sections of the new Roman Catholic ritual for anointing the sick. This Roman ritual is found on pages 93ff. of this book. We use the Roman ritual because it has evolved through 20 centuries, thus revealing the history of healing prayer, and because it includes prayers similar to those used by other Christian denominations. We hope that this view of the Rite and its history of healing prayer will enable individuals of all faiths to express better their own unique healing prayer.[1]

Since healing prayer is not limited to Roman Catholic priests ministering the Sacrament of Anointing, we will also explore what others, like Barbara who prays fruitfully for healing, have learned about healing prayer. They can assist all of us better to pray each part of the Rite so the sick will receive all the Lord's healing love; whether in the brief Rite of Anointing itself, or in its extension through healing prayer in the days that follow.

—Dennis

Chapter 1
Introductory Rite

During Carol's retreat, I directed her through the *Spiritual Exercises* of St. Ignatius. For 30 days I prayed and fasted, prayed and fasted; and for 30 days Carol prayed and fasted, prayed and fasted. The purpose of the retreat was to help Carol to know Jesus intimately so she would be willing to lay down everything for him. Though the experience of the retreat gave Carol the desire to do this, the experience of Jesus healing her deafness gave Carol an even greater desire to lay down everything for him.

Four hundred years ago when St. Francis Xavier wished to give non-Christian orientals a sense of intimacy with Jesus, he didn't start with a 30-day retreat. He trained the children in the village to pray for healing.[1] After training the children, Xavier would send them off to the villages to pray for their parents, relatives and friends. Those who were healed would then seek Xavier to find out how they could know the Healer more intimately, and many would eventually lay down everything to follow Jesus.

The introductory rite of the Roman ritual for anointing the sick declares what I discovered with Carol, and what Francis Xavier discovered with the children of India: Jesus answers the prayers of lay people when they pray for physical healing. Praying for physical healing is not limited to priests like Francis Xavier or to "professional people" such as faith healers and ministers. Rather, praying for physical healing is for ordinary people, lay people, friends or relatives, adults or children, or even one of the coastal fishermen, a corner prostitute or a tax collector whom Jesus asked to come follow him by healing in his name.

In recognizing that praying for physical healing belongs to priests as well as to lay people, the new Roman Rite for Anointing made two major changes: 1) Ideally, anointing is to be a *communal* rite utilizing not only the priest's but also the lay people's prayer power for healing. 2) Anointing is a rite for *healing* the sick rather than preparing the dying for death. Though the introductory rite includes only two parts, each part indicates one of those changes. In the first part, the greeting, the priest encourages all the lay people—including doctors, nurses, family, relatives and friends—to join their prayer power to heal. In the second part, the priest explains the Rite with a reading from James which indicates that the Rite's focus is not preparation for death but, rather, preparation for physical healing.

The old Rite stressed the priest's prayer for a happy death and not the lay people's prayer for healing. Remember the days when the priest came to anoint a sick relative? He came in the door, disappeared into the sick person's bedroom and left without saying a word. In the new Rite, the priest returns to early Christian tradition and invites the lay people to pray with him. The reading from James (5:13–16) states that when anyone is sick, the elders should pray over him. Though the "elders" who prayed with the sick may have at first been Christians designated by the community, within a few years not just elders but all family members were designated to pray for their sick. Centuries later, when a bishop questioned the current practice of lay anointing, Pope Innocent I (418 A.D.) declared that consecrated oil was to be used for healing by all Christians for "the needs of the members of their household."[2]

Unlike Baptism, Eucharist and Confession, during the first 400 years little attention was paid to the Rite of Anointing because all Christians, not just a priest, were generally involved. Frequently the oil was blessed at the Eucharist, then sent home and kept in the medicine cabinet. St. John Chrysostom couldn't keep oil in his sanctuary lamp because the people considered it blessed oil and kept taking it home to anoint their sick. This lay anointing continued through the eighth century, began to die off, but never totally died off until 1758. For example, the Council of Trent (c. 1550 AD) gave ecclesial approval to the lay anointing practiced in France and Italy. But approval stopped in 1758 when the Thomas Netter seminary textbook stated that previous textbook editions had erred in allowing laity to anoint the sick.[3]

Just as lay people are once again becoming ministers of the Eucharist, they may also again become ministers of the Sacrament of the Sick.[4] Though the priest presently administers the sacrament, lay people are once again given a central role as the priest encourages them to celebrate the Rite with him. All celebrating the Rite should "offer the sick love and help"[5] and should "pray with the sick"[6] both "before and after the celebration of the sacrament."[7] Because it is both prayer and their caring, loving presence which makes Christ's healing love tangible in this sacrament, those celebrating should approach "in a friendly manner."[8] The sacrament publicly celebrates and brings to the sick the loving, praying community of the Church that is present not just in the patient's room but in all parts of the world.

Anointing, like all other sacraments, publicly celebrates in a few moments what the Church expects us as Christians to do every moment of our lives. Thus a sacrament such as Reconciliation focuses on receiving forgiveness while a sacrament such as Matrimony focuses on giving of ourself completely to another person. But both the forgiveness and the giving of ourself completely to another need to be lived out in every moment of our life. The sacrament of Anointing ought to be lived out daily, not only by caring for the sick with a back rub or a phone call, but also by "praying with the sick" both "before and after the celebration of the sacrament."

Besides focusing on the role of the lay people, the new Rite also varies from the old Rite by emphasizing the healing of sickness rather than preparing the dying for death. The old rite was only given to people on their deathbed, and was even given to people who had already died. The U.S. Bishops' Conference made clear that the new Rite of Anointing is for the sick and that "the revised rite has removed the danger of death as a condition for the reception of the sacrament."[9] Since the new rite is about healing the sick, it is for those who are seriously

ill, and "there is no reason for scruples" in judging who
is seriously ill.[10] For example, the new rite is recom-
mended especially for older people in a weakened condition, although no dangerous illness is present.

The new rite's concern for physical healing is
evident in the reading from James 5:14–15, which explains:

> Is there anyone sick among you? Let him call
> for the elders of the church, and let them pray
> over him and anoint him in the name of the
> Lord. This prayer, made in faith, will save the
> sick man. The Lord will *restore* his health,
> and if he has committed any sins, they will be
> forgiven.

The writer of James states that the prayers for
healing will *restore* the sick man. "Restore" *(egerein)*,
when used in New Testament times, refers to physical
healing (e.g., Mt 9:5–7; Mk 1:31; Acts 3:7), even bringing back to life one who had died. Physical healing was
foremost in the thoughts of the early fathers when they
prayed for the sick with blessings based on James. All 13
blessings of oil still in existence from that period mention
physical healing. The five most ancient blessings for the
sick mention only physical healing and do not explicitly
refer to spiritual effects. The Greek Church has retained
this focus through the centuries and, even today, emphasizes physical healing through anointing with oil.

Only after the eighth century was anointing with
oil used mainly for the dying rather than as a means for
physical healing of the sick. Why this gradual shift from
the lay people praying with the sick for physical healing,
to the priests praying with the dying for a happy death?

Among the many reasons are, first, a desire for redemptive suffering rather than for healing; second, a delay in the anointing until deathbed confession and, third, lay abuses of oil.

First, Christians prayed less for physical healing and more for redemptive suffering when the age of martyrdom ceased. Unfortunately for healing, Emperor Constantine (c. 300 A.D.) made Christianity the official religion of the Roman Empire, thus stopping the flow of martyr's blood. Since they could no longer die for Christ, Christians gave their bodies to Christ when suffering illness. There soon developed a theology of illness as redemptive suffering, ignoring prayer for healing of illness.

Second, after the fifth century, confession of sins gradually became a requirement when priests ministered the sacrament of anointing. Since the church imposed extreme confessional penances (e.g. to spend years fasting or in a monastery), most people put off confession and anointing by a priest until they had dug their graves. Even after penances were relaxed and confession became more frequent, people still clung to the old practice of waiting until death to be anointed by a priest.

Third, because of abuses, by the ninth century lay people lost most privileges of anointing with oil. As martyrs became more rare, veneration for them increased, and Christians felt unworthy to pray for healing unless at a martyr's shrine or using martyr's relics. Soon the selling of spiritual favors and oil at these shrines grew into a profitable business, attracting greedy merchants or leading to superstitious practices. In an effort to stop these abuses, the use of oil was more and more restricted to the clergy, especially through the eighth century Carolingian reform. Furthermore, the prayers for anointing the sick were inserted unfortunately in many Carolingian rituals right after deathbed penance, thus, again, linking anointing with praying for the dying.

But today in the new Rite, since anointing is no longer associated with praying for the dying, we are again invited to join the priest in using our prayer power for physical healing. In praying for physical healing, we are responding to the promise Jesus extended to us, "they will lay their hands on the sick, who will recover" (Mark 16:18).

Unfortunately, we sometimes believe, as St. Augustine did, that only first-century Christianity needed the witness value of physical healing. But two years after Augustine drew this conclusion, he had witnessed 70 healings in his own church, and this forced him to retract his previous statement and to proclaim that healing was indeed meant for his own fourth century Christians. In inviting all to pray for physical healing, the intoductory rite declares with Augustine that healing is for all Christians, whether they belong to the fourth or twentieth century, just as it was for Christians of the first century.

—Dennis

For more than a dozen years the Lord has been teaching me about my responsibility as a lay person to pray for the sick. My book, *Healing Prayer* describes my first feeble attempts in exercising the commission Jesus gave to "whoever believes in me." There is little room for excusing ourselves when we take John 14:12 literally, and accept the fact that we are called to do the same works as Jesus. "I tell you most solemnly, whoever believes in me will perform the same works as I do myself, he will perform even greater works, because I am going to the Father." Throughout the Acts of the Apostles we encounter early Christians continuing to heal the sick, as Jesus did, especially those who were lame and paralyzed. My experience has shown me that these "acts" are supposed to continue in today's church through the hands and hearts of lay people who have accepted Jesus as their Lord and Savior.

Many lay people attend religious services, but seldom realize their role in bringing healing to others because they consider themselves inadequate, unworthy, unspiritual or too sinful to ever be an instrument of the Lord. One wonders what would happen if all who call themselves Christian decided to exercise their spiritual gifts on a given Sunday morning. The power of atomic energy would pale in comparison!

I often hear from Christians who have found themselves in situations where they prayed with another, out of sheer desperation, only to discover God answering in very profound ways. One such incident involved a delivery room nurse who assisted at the birth of a one-and-one-half-pound premature stillborn baby boy. The infant was placed in a basinet while the nurses finished caring for the mother and returning her to the ward. Nearly 10 minutes had passed since the delivery, but the R.N., who had never prayed over anyone, began to feel that she should lay hands on the baby and ask the Lord to give him life. It seemed so ridiculous, since the doctor had already signed the death certificate, and the infant had been without oxygen for so long, but there was no one else who could intercede at that moment.

The nurse placed her hands on the tiny baby and asked Jesus to bless his lifeless form. Within seconds he began to breathe, moving his arms and legs. She quickly took him into the nursery where he was placed in an isolette and continued to make remarkable progress. After a year's time, the child appears to be developing normally, and the nurse is still awed at this amazing response to prayer.

A good place to begin exercising our ability to pray with one another is in our own homes. The Christian family is a community which is designed to exemplify the love of Jesus for his church, as St. Paul describes it in Ephesians 5:23. The relationship of husband and wife is to be a "great foreshadowing" of the intimacy between the Lord and his people. Therefore, family members should be natural channels of healing for one another. Married couples can do themselves, and their children, a great favor if they undertake to pray together on a regular basis, asking God's blessing on one another and their households. Parents are wonderful instruments of healing for their children, even if they have never attended a workshop on the subject. It seems only logical that the Lord, who entrusted us with the responsibility of rearing youngsters, would also aid us in the process when we invoke his help.

There is a particular role of guardianship assigned to fathers, which makes it imperative that they never underestimate the necessity of interceding for the family. St. Joseph received a warning in a dream to protect Jesus by a journey to Egypt and, still today, God continues to bless the homes where fathers exercise their protective capacity.

Scripture relates the story of a synagogue chief, Jairus, who begs Jesus to come to his home because his

12-year-old daughter lay dying (Lk 8:40–56). By the time they arrived at the home, the mourners were wailing over the girl's body. Therefore, Jesus sent everyone away except Peter, James, John and the *girl's parents*. Undoubtedly they were a healthy influence because the girl returned to life and the Lord told them to give her something to eat. Perhaps Jairus and his wife will inspire more parents to become channels for their children's wholeness.

My friends, Kathy and Tom O'Regan of Highland Park, Illinois, are a beautiful example of a couple who understand this principle. Their young son, Joey, was born with multiple birth defects, i.e., cleft palate, cleft lip, hip deformities, heart murmur. From the moment of his birth, Joey's parents have surrounded him with loving prayer; the kind of intercession Fr. Francis MacNutt describes as "soaking prayer."[11] As a result, one hip has spontaneously healed, he has shown remarkable recuperative ability through his various surgeries, and maintains a joyful disposition which draws people to him. Kathy and Tom have found their love for each other has increased as they've joined together to minister to their little son.

Children can also be wonderful channels of healing love for their parents, as witnessed by the following illustration sent to me by Thea Connally of Palatine, Illinois.

> "I had been sick for 18 years, having spent four months in the National Institute of Health, blind, crippled and with a rare skin disease. I had been in a wheel chair on and off, blind, on and off, had stomach ulcers, kidney infections, rheumatoid arthritis in

every joint of my body. My eyes hemorrhaged and I developed cysts and boils within and without my body. The last three years of having these diseases, my venal system was being destroyed and I would get blood clots in both legs. I coughed up blood now and then, and was severely anemic. I was told that my bone marrow was not producing sufficient amounts of new blood cells to keep me alive. I would need transfusions because any form of iron, taken orally, was radically destroying my stomach with ulcers. I was allergic to everything but sleep.

"My four children were becoming belligerent, rebellious and cynical. It was necessary for them to do so much that there wasn't much time or joy for them. I tried desperately to hide my feelings, but despair, guilt and frustration would burst forth on the children in one form or another.

"One day my 14-year-old son came home from some meeting and said that he'd been baptized in the Holy Spirit. With that statement I thought a heart attack or stroke would be added to my already numerous diseases. I said, 'Our church preaches only one baptism. What have you done?' He very patiently and lovingly showed me in scripture where this baptism of the Holy Spirit is. He convinced me that he was not going to hell for this. Week by week I saw him change as he consistently reacted with love and obedience. He spoke of a real living Jesus who was changing his life. I felt like an ogre in the light of his love.

"One day, after hearing more bad news regarding some of my tests, I was in the living room crying for three hours. I didn't know how to prepare my children for living without me. I had two sons, 14 and 9, and two daughters, 12 and 3. My 14-year-old son came home from school and saw me crying. He knew what I was going through. He held my arm and as he prayed aloud for me, I felt a strange, awesome sensation, I stopped crying and felt at peace. Something good but unexplainable was happening to me."

This young boy's prayer on behalf of his mother enabled her to begin attending prayer meetings where she received further ministering until, after a year's time, she was pronounced totally healed by her doctors. Every laboratory test was normal and Thea was able to assume a normal, productive life. She and her husband, Ralph, have gone on to develop their own ministry to the sick. All this proceeded from the effects of a youngster's petition for his mother.

The greeting in the new rite invites all people to use the healing power of Jesus Christ in praying for the needs of others.

May we each accept that invitation.

—Barbara

Chapter 2
Penitential Rite

After the introduction, the Rite of the Sick provides an opportunity to ask for forgiveness. Since the prayers ask God to forgive *us*—not just *me*, we must be willing not only to receive God's forgiveness but also to extend his complete forgiveness toward all. Likewise to the degree that those praying for the sick can forgive one another, their prayer has more love power (Mk 11:25). Lack of forgiveness toward others and toward God seems to be the most common obstacle to healing. When we resent another we also close our heart to the loving Christ present in that person. Similarly, until we ask forgiveness for hurting Christ present in another, we erect a barrier to receiving his healing love. What we do to the least of our brothers, we do to Jesus, and thereby either invite or block his healing love. To aid reconciliation many priests, before starting the penitential rite, pause to let the sick person recall who has hurt him the most and, thus, most needs his forgiveness.

Throughout history, Christians have recognized the need to forgive and be forgiven as a preparation for healing. Jesus prepared the paralytic to walk by first forgiving his deeper sinful paralysis (Mk 2:1-12). James 5:15-16 stressed that the sick man's sins would be forgiven. St. Bede (735 A.D.) cited both James' epistle and Innocent I's decree that penitents should not be anointed for healing until they were forgiven.

As mentioned in the previous chapter, with the passage of time, more stress was placed on confessing sins to a priest until anointing finally became associated with deathbed confession. However, the new Rite recommends sacramental confession as a means of healing and recommends that "whenever it is necessary, the priest should hear the sacramental confession of the sick person, if possible, before the celebration of anointing."[1] Sacramental confession would be particularly healing for those experiencing heavy guilt or a deep awareness of having harmed the Christian community.[2]

Even an apparently insignificant sin, such as lying to a friend, spreads and festers into deceit-filled Watergates and wars. Through sacramental confession the priest extends to us the forgiveness of the entire community, bringing peace to our spirits. In situations where sacramental confession is not used, the penitential rite is prayed in order that we can declare our sinfulness and receive forgiveness from one another.

St. Bede suggests, along with James, that even those praying for the sick man are to confess their daily sins to one another, enabling them to become better channels for Christ's healing love. When we give a workshop on healing, we find the best preparation is to confess our sins to each other, especially any misunderstandings which may have hurt one another. When we do that, we clear the channels for healing to happen through us.

Not only Christian tradition but also modern medicine teaches the power of healing through forgiveness. Since Dr. Walter Cannon, in 1914, measured the physiological changes in a cat experiencing anger and fear stimulated by a barking dog, researchers have probed the body's "fight-flight" response triggered by fear, anger or the self-anger of guilt.[3] An ulcer patient will have his ulcers recur unless, through forgiveness, he deals with the hurts outside himself that create anger, and the hurts within himself that create guilt. The heart patient must also deal with the free-floating anger of his "type-A behavior" that pressures him to do more in less time.[4] Anger and guilt also play a role in triggering or aggravating neurodermatitis, hypertension, asthma, migraines, colitis, rheumatoid arthritis and a host of other illnesses. We also know that a body free from excessive anger, fear and guilt heals faster and is more immune to illness.[5]

The Our Father's "forgive us our trespasses as we forgive those who trespass against us" illuminates the Lord's way to heal the fear, anger and guilt which provide a breeding ground for illness. Fears disappear when we get angry enough to attack the fears outside of ourselves, and guilty enough to face the fears within ourselves. It helps little to take the fear of losing our job and replace this fear with anger against the boss, or with guilt that paralyzes us by making us focus on our errors.

The Our Father tells us not only to change what we can to make the Kingdom come, but also to forgive the boss who hurt us and to ask forgiveness from God and

from those wounded by our errors. Forgiveness of others
deals with anger. Forgiveness of ourselves deals with the
guilt that, together with anger, breeds and prolongs illness.

Sin, with its accompanying feelings of anger and
guilt, often but not always, becomes a factor in illness.
Christ pointed out that neither the blind man nor his
parents had sinned (Jn 9:3). Often the sin belongs to
others: the greedy polluting factories belching fourth
cancerous fumes, the inadequate wages and health care
we offer the poor, our lack of care and prayer for the
sick, our inability to help another before his burdens lead
to a heart attack.

As Dr. Hans Selye showed, stress is a factor in
nearly every illness, and we make one another ill to the
degree that we create stress in our environment or fail to
relieve it.[6] Maybe that's why James (5:14–16) suggests
that those who pray for the sick confess their sins to one
another, enabling them to pray the heartfelt prayer of a
good man.

While living with the Sioux Indians, who were
under constant stress from their poverty and disintegrat-
ing culture, we came to appreciate the importance of
dealing with stress in order to assure continued healing.
We noticed how many Sioux were healed of arthritis and
ulcers through prayer while attending conferences away
from the sufferings of the reservation, only to have the
symptoms recur following the return to their stressful
environment, where there is about 70% unemployment
and rampant alcoholism.

However, if they found jobs, their husbands quit
drinking, or their marriages were reconciled, they could
be prayed with and, this time, remain free from

rheumatoid arthritis or ulcers. For healing prayer to be more effective, we must all confess our failure to make the love of Christ more present in our environment and, with the help of Jesus, change what can be changed. We give the daily bread of health when we can say: "forgive us our trespasses as we forgive those who trespass against us."

—Matt and Dennis

The first step in anointing always involves removing the sin from our lives before we can obtain a blessing. The same pattern can be seen in the liturgy, when we ask for forgiveness before we proceed with the celebration. There does not seem to be any greater deterrent to wholeness than a lack of forgiveness in our lives and, no matter how we try to justify our position, it remains an unavoidable obstacle.

We have encountered numerous persons who experienced healing after they forgave others, God or themselves. In March, 1976, Matt, Dennis and I prayed with a Canadian priest with a diagnosed slipped disc, which made it difficult for him to walk and impossible for him to bend over. This condition persisted for two years until. . . .

> "Last night I sat there, and it was a humiliation to sit in front of all of you. I was asked to pull my shirt up (so doctors could check his spine), and that was the ultimate. I said to the Lord, 'Here I am making a fool of myself, but I believe.' So they began to pray and pray and

nothing happened to me except a great peace. Then someone said, 'John, forgive and fill your heart with forgiveness.' I really felt that I had forgiven everyone, but I began going over, one-by-one, the people who had hurt me, forgave them again and, immediately, things began to happen.

"There was a hand touching me right at the bottom of my back, and immediately electricity passed from that hand and began soaking into my spine. It hurt a little bit, like when you have surgery for a cyst, which I had just undergone. You don't feel the pain because of the anesthesia, but you feel the pulling—and there was pulling going on in my back. That curve is not there any more. Walking, I felt very clumsy on my feet—now I am more steady. I keep saying: 'Lord, you are tremendous!' I really want to thank all who prayed for me because I really felt the body of Christ there, and I felt your love and compassion which was very strong. Jesus was as real there as he was in Galilee, and he touched me through you."

John's healed spine was immediately confirmed by several doctors who had helped us with the prayer. Two years later, John is still totally healed. Forgiveness seems to be one of the most common ways to trigger the Lord's healing power.

Sometimes forgiveness seems nearly impossible because we associate forgiveness with a "feeling" of love toward another. Though this may happen as forgiveness deepens, forgiveness usually begins by deciding to cease harboring anger towards another or guilt towards ourself. This act of our will opens the door of our spirit to enable the Lord to begin to bless our lives. Healing often occurs when we begin exercising this discipline of forgiveness.

Though it may be easy for us to understand the need of forgiving ourself or another person, many Christians have difficulty understanding why it might be necessary, or even possible, for them to forgive God. Of course he is sinless, and we are not denying the perfection of his will for us. What we are recognizing is our own imperfections in perceiving his love for us, and the times we have misinterpreted the Father's actions. Perhaps the following excerpt from a letter written to me by Margaret Cossentino, a registered nurse, will illustrate this point:

> "When I arrived at the retreat on Friday evening, I was in quite a bit of pain. Two weeks before the weekend I had a miscarriage at 3 months and developed phlebitis in my left leg. During the Friday night session in the Chapel, I was able to 'forgive God' for this miscarriage, allowing his healing love to replace the anger and resentment I felt toward him. What a tremendous relief it was for me! Early Saturday morning, about 3:30 a.m., I awoke with the feeling I should be praying. Soon I realized I was sitting Indian-style on the bed and was comfortable. I got up and walked on my leg which was no longer painful. In fact, I jumped up and down to see if it would hurt and it didn't. I should have told you about it then, but I was a little skeptical as to how long it would last since this was my second bout with phlebitis. Now it has been seven months and I have not had a twinge of discomfort in my leg."

It is not uncommon for us to erect barriers in our relationship with the Lord, although they are often so subtle we fail to recognize them. Admitting our honest feelings enables us to discover anew the tremendous love our Father has for his rebellious children.

The penitential rite offers us an opportunity to confess our faults and receive absolution for the sins we've committed. Guilt can and does have a definite effect on our physical condition as Psalm 32 attests:

> "Happy the man whom Yahweh
>   accuses of no guilt,
>   whose spirit is incapable of deceit!
> All the time I kept silent, my bones were
>   wasting away
>   with groans, day in, day out;
> day and night your hand
>   lay heavy on me;
> my heart grew parched as stubble
>   in summer drought.
> At last I admitted to you I had sinned;
>   no longer concealing my guilt,
> I said, 'I will go to Yahweh
>   and confess my fault'.
> And you, you have forgiven the wrong I did,
>   have pardoned my sin."

I recall praying with a young woman who had suffered from constant migraine headaches for several years. The onset of the condition occurred immediately after she had undergone a medical abortion for a three-month pregnancy. She convinced herself that the abortion was justified, even bragged about the operation, but her body was contradicting the rationale. She finally agreed to seek out a priest, went to confession and her migraines completely disappeared. She later told me that it wasn't difficult to believe God could forgive her failing, but she had a terrific battle learning to forgive herself.

As we can see, the penitential rite in the Sacrament of the Sick is very important to the one receiving the prayer.

—Barbara

Chapter 3
Scripture Reading

The third section of the Rite of Anointing designates that a suitable passage from scripture be read by the priest or one of those present. This practice finds its roots not only in Jesus, who began his Galilean healing ministry by reading from Isaiah (Lk 4:18–19), but also in first-century Christian communities which used James 5:14–16 as they prayed for healing. We have chosen a passage from John's Gospel:

> I tell you most solemnly,
> whoever believes in me
> will perform the same works as I do myself,
> he will perform even greater works,
> because I am going to the Father.
> Whatever you ask for in my name I will do,
> so that the Father may be glorified in the Son.
> If you ask for anything in my name,
> I will do it.
>
> (Jn 14: 12–14)

Why then doesn't more happen when we ask for healing in Jesus name? Christ is so eager to heal that he healed even on the Sabbath, and healed without being asked, though he knew it meant the authorities would plot to kill him (Mk 3:1-6; Jn 5:1-18). He was just as eager for his disciples to heal the sick and his last words recorded in Mark are, "And these signs will accompany those who believe. . . .they will lay their hands upon the sick and they will recover" (Mk 16:17-18). If Christ is so eager to heal through us, why doesn't it happen more often in prayer?

Jesus promised: "Whatever you ask in my name, I will do it." Prayer often seems futile, because to ask "in the name of Jesus, heal Ann," may not really be asking in Jesus' name. To the Jew the name signified everything about a person's character. Therefore, asking in Jesus' name would mean asking with the Lord's thoughts and feelings, just as Christ would. When we are asking for the healing the Lord wishes, Jesus promises to answer our prayer. The scripture reading of Jesus' healing comes early in the Rite so we can put on the mind and heart of Christ to pray in his name. We should also pray for Jesus' mind to guide us in the choice of a scripture passage that will speak directly to the sick person's needs.

If we don't see our prayer being answered, it is often because we are focusing on our way rather than praying in the name of Jesus, with his mind and heart, seeking his way and time. Sometimes we are asking for an ulcer to be healed, and missing how Christ first desires to heal the circumstances so the ulcer won't recur.

How do we know the way in which Christ wishes to heal? The challenge is not to have more faith in our faith, but to have enough love so we can see the more loving way Jesus wishes to heal. We come before Jesus and silently listen to the way he is speaking of his love for his loved one. Sickness and pain are usually not Jesus' will because they leave a wake of self-centeredness, making it difficult to love God, others and ourselves. Whenever this occurs, we can be sure that Jesus wants to heal the illness or at least heal the way it chokes our power to love.

Some people have a rare vocation to suffer redemptively and to grow in their power to love as they endure their illness. When working as an orderly, Matt cared for a saintly Dominican, Fr. Paschal Kelly, who suffered for 20 years from multiple sclerosis, despite prayer for healing. He would lie in bed, not able to turn his head or scratch a maddening itch.

Despite the fact that Fr. Kelly was confined to a hospital, Matt relates that ''many people from all over the world—including Hollywood stars—came to see him. What they came to witness was how Fr. Kelly's suffering made him like Jesus. I would put him into a wheelchair and take him to visit the sickest, most depressed patient. It was difficult for any patient to feel sorry for himself after seeing Fr. Kelly, smiling from his wheelchair.''

What Matt witnessed was this priest's ability to reach the poor, the lonely and those who felt abandoned, because he experienced utter dependence on the love of our heavenly Father. This type of suffering is redemptive to the degree that it leads us to give and receive the Lord's love. Suffering is redemptive if it is healing.

Finally, some people are to become like Christ, not through the ordinary way of healing or the rarer way

of redemptive suffering, but through the ultimate healing, death, with its gift of a resurrected and healed body.
There is a time to pray, not for healing, but for relief of
pain and a happy death.

How do we know whether it is God's will or a
suicidal wish for a person to die? We wouldn't pray for
death if a person is depressed or desiring death because
he is tortured by pain or a problem. We would first pray
for relief of the pain, problem or depression, so that a
person can choose death, not because he is running from
something painful, but because he is running toward
God. If a dying person is choosing God rather than running from life, then we are often led to pray for a happy
death.

Whether we are praying for death or for life, our
prayer becomes more powerful as we become a channel
of Christ's love. People in love don't just say "I love
you," they daydream about each other. Deep love is
deeper than conscious words and flows into the imagination to influence the subconscious. Healing prayer, too,
should utilize the imagination to remove the subconscious blocks to Christ's healing love.[1] Picturing the person whole lets Christ give his healing love through our
subconscious imagination, and deepens our own trust in
his love. This also helps the sick person. The patient who
imagines himself getting well generally heals faster.

Dr. Carl Simonton, a leading oncologist, finds
that hopeless cases of cancer often go into remission once
the patient can imagine and believe his phagocytes are
like fish eating the cancer cells and bringing health.[2]
Every basketball player knows how to make more bas-
kets by imagining the free throw splitting the net rather
than bouncing off the rim. Praying in Jesus' name means

removing subconscious barriers by imagining the healing already taking place.

For a long time we avoided imagining and describing the healing we thought Jesus wanted for fear of raising false hopes. Now we simply let the sick person know that the way we imagine healing may fall short of God's perfect plan, but we must always be ready to accept his more loving way and moment, which is infinitely beyond what we can ask for or imagine (Eph 3:20). Listening to the scriptures thus leads us all to pray in Christ's name—as Jesus would ask the Father. The Father will answer our prayer because the voice crying out is Jesus' voice inside of us.

—*Matt and Dennis*

Scripture reading is an integral part of every sacrament, reminding us that the bible continues to be the "living word of God." Roman Catholics are becoming more familiar with scripture, particularly through the encouragement and teaching in the Charismatic renewal. This is enabling us to learn to know God's plan of salvation in a much deeper way.

The Gospel narratives give us a graphic picture of the Lord's approach to sickness, since the majority of his public life was devoted to healing. Jesus had overwhelming compassion for those who were suffering, and was constantly reaching out to bring wholeness.

A sick person can receive much comfort from reading the bible, and often discovers renewed faith in the Father's love as the living word touches his spirit. I have heard countless testimonies from people whose illness began to disappear as they invoked the power of a scripture passage.

Many times I've encouraged a person to imagine himself in a particular Gospel episode and "see" Jesus ministering his healing love in today's situation. God's attitude toward sickness is the same as it was 2000 years ago, and he continues to respond with the same touch of love when we call upon the Lord.

If someone is incapacitated and unable to read the bible, we can perform a great service by reading it to him. This is an apostolate which many volunteer visitors to the sick should consider adding to their duties.

A person in a coma is often able to hear what is being said, even if unable to respond in a visible way. This is why it is so important that only positive, affirming words are spoken at the bedside of an unconscious patient, giving him messages of life and hope.

People who have survived comatose states will often be able to relate entire conversations which went on in their rooms while they were seemingly unaware. Many times such persons have related to me the tremendous effect the word of God had upon them in their helpless condition. One woman who survived a severe auto accident declared, "I was given the courage to live when I heard my sister repeatedly saying 'I can do all things through Christ who strengthens me'" (Ph 4:13 RSV).

One dramatic example of healing through scripture happened to a man who suffered a massive stroke and was pronounced in a vegetative state by his physicians. After several weeks he was moved to a nursing home where the staff was instructed to make his lifeless body as comfortable as possible. His wife visited him every day, and for hours would sit by his bedside reading the bible to him. Within six weeks he began to show signs of improvement as his spouse continued her daily vigil and local prayer groups began to lend their support. It was a day for much celebration when he walked out of the nursing home, showing only the slightest residual effects from his former condition, and praising God that his word was true.

The Rite of Anointing instructs the priest to choose a reading suitable for the occasion in order to focus our attention on the presence of Jesus in our midst.

—Barbara

Chapter 4
Litany

Lord, through this holy anointing, come
and comfort __N__ with your love and mercy.
>   **R.** Lord, hear our prayer.

Free __N__ from all harm.
>   **R.** Lord, hear our prayer.

Relieve the sufferings of all the sick
(here present).
>   **R.** Lord, hear our prayer.

Assist all those dedicated to the care of
the sick.
>   **R.** Lord, hear our prayer.

Free __N__ from sin and all temptation.
>   **R.** Lord, hear our prayer.

Give life and health to our brother (sister)
__N__, on whom we lay our hands in your
>   name.
>   **R.** Lord, hear our prayer.

In this section of the Rite of Anointing, we begin to pray as did Christ and the early Christians. Though we do not have any Western liturgical formula for anointing until after 800 A.D., we do have litanies which early Christians may have used at the time of anointing such as "bless all who live here" or "bless this dwelling." The early Christians didn't have books with printed responses to prayers, so they used a litany form of short requests, each followed by a set response such as "Lord, hear our prayer," or "Lord, have mercy." The sick, who didn't have the strength or the attention to say long prayers, could pray the litany by simply responding "Lord, hear our prayer" to whatever prayer the healthy and creative leader composed. The current litany in the Anointing of the Sick, again, gives the sick a chance to pray for themselves, for others who are sick, and especially for those "who care for the sick."

The heartfelt prayer of the sick has great power to help others. When working as a hospital chaplain, Matt would ask someone suffering great pain from surgery to pray for another near death. Very often the dying person would take a sudden turn toward recovery, or else request that Matt come to help prepare him for death.

"One man, Bill, wanted nothing to do with religion until Bertha, in pain from gall bladder surgery, spent a sleepless night praying for him." Explained Matt: "About 3:00 AM, Bill called for me, and he died receiving the Lord's forgiveness and peace. Bertha also offered her pain and prayers for Mary, a 68-year-old widow barely alive and needing gall bladder surgery. Through the skills of the doctors and prayers of Bertha, Mary recovered in record time and with little pain. A patient in pain can pray with deep empathetic power for another to recover and be freed from pain."

Whether using the formal litanies or other informal prayers, the sick may themselves be healed as they intercede for others. Kathy, for example, was in fine shape, walking through the woods to our healing conference, when she dislocated her toe. An orthopedic surgeon at the conference tried, unsuccessfully, to manipulate the toe back into place. We all prayed for Kathy and felt confident that the Lord would remove the pain so she could pray and focus on the healing conference. To our surprise, nothing happened.

That night Kathy was hobbling along with a friend to get some things from her car. As she opened the car door she accidentally slammed it shut on her friend's hand. Immediately Kathy, with her throbbing foot, knew her friend's pain and prayed that Jesus might heal the hand. The pain left the hand while, at the same time, Kathy's dislocated toe popped back in place. In reaching out to heal another, Kathy was healed.

During the same workshop, another lady tore a knee cartilege which locked her leg so she couldn't straighten it out. The orthopedic surgeon diagnosed this as probably requiring surgery. We asked her to pray in her pain for those desiring physical healing. Not only were many physically healed by her heartfelt prayer but, by the next morning, her own knee was healed. Now in our workshops those with similar ailments are asked to pray with one another since they really understand the suffering and, often, receive healing while in prayer for a fellow sufferer. As promised long ago in Isaiah 58:6-8, when reaching out to help another, "your wound shall quickly be healed."

—Matt and Dennis

The litany in the Rite of Anointing invites everyone, including the sick person, to join the priest in prayer,
becoming actively involved in the sacrament. The one
who is ill can petition God's mercy for himself, his loved
ones and the medical personnel caring for him. This provides a marvelous opportunity to receive the Lord's
blessings. Countless people have been healed through
this unselfish love ''because the amount you measure out
is the amount you will be given back'' (Lk 6:38). As the
patient reaches out in loving concern to pray for the needs
of those around him, Jesus reaches in to answer the sick
person's own desires.

I think it is especially appropriate that the sick
person intercedes for the doctors, hospital staff, family
and friends who are ministering to him. The person who
is ill does himself a great favor when he prays for those
who are caring for his physical needs, asking that their
hands become the healing hands of Jesus Christ bringing
wholeness. He should ask for the gift of wisdom to be
given to his physicians so they properly diagnose and
treat his illness. There are hundreds of people behind the
scenes in every hospital (in laboratories, kitchens, main-
tenance, laundry) who would also appreciate being
blessed through a patient's prayers. The litany affords an
opportunity to do that very thing.

The healing love of Jesus can be more fully experienced when people unite in prayer for the one who is
sick. As we join our hearts in harmony with other believ-
ers, we discover the truth of the words of Jesus: ''If two
of you on earth agree to ask anything at all, it will be
granted to you by my Father in heaven'' (Mt 18:19). We
sometimes discover rapid answers to our prayers when
we submit the requests to fellow Christians and stop try-

ing to carry the full weight of intercession. The phenomenal rise in the number of prayer groups throughout the world, even Protestant and Catholics praying together in war-torn Northern Ireland, gives witness to the fact that people have a deep longing to share prayer with each other.

Recently I was asked to pray with a woman hospitalized in the terminal stages of cancer. She was in constant pain with the prospect of death creating a tremendous anxiety. Several of her relatives were present in the hospital room, so I invited them to speak to the Lord concerning Betty's need for wholeness. They were somewhat self-conscious, but one, then another, began to ask Jesus to touch their beloved relative. Their discomfort quickly turned to serenity as the presence of the Lord descended upon the entire gathering. Betty's physical pain completely subsided and, within a few days, she died peacefully in her sleep.

Her sister phoned to thank me for giving the family an opportunity to pray. "We were all praying for Betty individually," she said, "but none of us had realized the importance of praying together *with* her. The experience has deepened our relationship with God and with one another."

—Barbara

Chapter 5
Laying On of Hands

The laying on of hands is a rite of healing touch practiced by the earliest Christians as they prayed over the sick (Jas 5:14). Jesus frequently used touch to heal and told his followers that "they will lay hands upon the sick, who will recover" (Mk 16:18). Thus Paul was healed of blindness as Ananias laid hands on him (Acts 9:17). To the Jew, touch bestowed one's power just as Moses laid his hand and power on Joshua (Nm 27:18–20), or as Jesus felt power go out from him when touched by the woman with the hemorrhage (Lk 8:46). Touch remained important even to the early church, as exemplified by St. Irenaeus (150 A.D.) who reports that he and others "still heal the sick by laying hands on them and they are made whole."[1]

Touch is a natural healing gift and, like all natural gifts, the Lord can use it just as he makes a gift for preaching out of the natural gift for speaking. Dr. Dolores Kreiger, professor at New York University, has taught 3,000 doctors, nurses and therapists how to lay hands lovingly on their patients and thus transmit healing energy from themselves to a sick person whose illness has placed him or her in an energy "deficit."[2] Dr. Kreiger has been able to demonstrate clinically the effectiveness of touch by measuring a significant rise in hemoglobin levels in the patients who receive this treatment.

Touch can even make the difference between death and life. During World War II, orphaned English babies often died after being institutionalized, with the exception of one orphanage where a night worker lovingly held the lonely babies after finishing her cleaning tasks. Now, in every maternity ward, nurses routinely give babies one of the most powerful forms of medicine, a loving hug. Likewise, mothers are encouraged to touch a child after birth and to breastfeed the baby, not only because mother's milk is healthy, but because a mother's touch brings comfort and security. Some psychologists report that children who are not lovingly touched have a much higher incidence of schizophrenia, because they are verbally told they are loved but not tactually shown it.

Does our puritanical inhibition against touching another person also inhibit the flow of the Spirit's healing power, which was so evident in the early church? Laying on of hands should be a natural gesture communicating the care, gentleness and strength of Christ sending his Spirit to heal. Likewise, allowing another to touch you is a natural gesture showing openness and acceptance. Laying on of hands is such an ancient and powerful gesture that every sacrament but Matrimony utilizes it to confer the Holy Spirit's power.[3]

In the Rite of Anointing, hands are *silently* laid

upon the sick because we are not praying our own individual healing prayer; rather, our hands have become the
hands of Jesus and his church, praying in the Spirit for
healing. When praying over another, we try to imagine
how Jesus would lovingly touch this person, asking the
Lord's presence to flow through our hands. It's like the
image of the roadside crucifix in France which was missing the Lord's hands due to the bombing of World War
II. Someone who understood the laying on of hands
placed on the cross, "I have no hands but yours." Often
with touch alone we can communicate Christ's love in
ways beyond words. The important thing is to become a
channel of God's healing love so the sick person can feel
"only Jesus."

—Matt and Dennis

The importance of touch has been given quite a lot
of publicity in recent years. In my area of the country you
often see the bumper sticker, "Have you hugged your kid
today?"—courtesy of the local mental health society. I
suggest they amend the question to read, "Have you
hugged *anyone* today?", since we all need these outward
signs of affection, no matter how old we are.

The laying on of hands provides us with an occasion to demonstrate our concern for another person as we
reach out to make a physical connection, just as the kiss
of peace at Mass becomes a time for affirming community through touch. Our hands communicate volumes of
non-verbal information as we discover when shaking
hands with someone. Many businessmen can accurately

predict a person's character through the ritual of the handshake.

The scriptures are filled with accounts of the beneficial effects of the laying on of hands as practiced by Jesus and his disciples. Besides demonstrating a loving concern, there is often a transference of power as we ask Jesus to permit our hands to be channels of his love. Many people experience a feeling of heat, tingling of nerves or slight vibrations as they pray over another. These same phenomena are also reported by the individuals receiving prayer, which makes the theory of energy-flow a possibility. Many scientific experiments are now being conducted to prove such a force exists but, with or without the proof, the results speak for themselves.

A typical letter reads;

"I had never before been 'prayed over' with the laying on of hands until the night of my first prayer meeting. The priest leading the group asked if anyone needed physical healing, and I was experiencing severe back pain due to a fall several years ago. I sat in the chair and a few members from the group laid hands on my back and began to quietly pray. It was as if an electric current went right through my spine and all the pain subsided. What a relief to be able to move about without excruciating suffering! I knew it was Jesus who touched me that night through the hands of those beautiful people, and I will be eternally grateful."

The new Rite of Anointing incorporates the laying on of hands into the ritual in order that the blessing might flow through the entire body of the sick person. We are not only concerned with the salvation of his soul, but also with the restoration of his body and this gesture symbolizes that truth. Jesus healed the *total person* as he walked upon this earth and, through our loving touch, he continues to free his people.

—Barbara

Chapter 6
Blessing of Oil

Just as Jesus uses the touch of loving hands to enable us to feel his healing love, so, too, he places his power in oil which tells all our senses that he is healing the whole person. The prayer for blessing this oil not only recognizes the need to expect healing of body, mind and soul, but also encourages us to treat and pray for the whole sick person. Members of the early church believed that this prayer, which is based on the bishop's *"Emitte"* prayer recorded by Hippolytus in 197 A.D., consecrated the oil with divine power so that anyone could use it with the deep expectation for healing.[1] Today the bishop consecrates the oil of the sick during Holy Thursday's Eucharist immediately before the doxology, when we offer ourselves and our gifts to the Father through Jesus and the Spirit. Priests, too, by saying the following prayer of the bishop can consecrate oil for the sacrament of the sick.

Let us pray.

Lord God, loving Father,
you bring healing to the sick
through your Son Jesus Christ.
Hear us as we pray to you in faith,
and send the Holy Spirit, man's
    Helper and Friend,
upon this oil, which nature has provided
to serve the needs of men.
May your blessing +
come upon all who are anointed
with this oil,
that they may be freed from pain
    and illness
and made well again in body, mind,
    and soul.
Father, may this oil be blessed for
    our use
in the name of our Lord Jesus Christ
who lives and reigns with you for
    ever and ever.
    R. Amen.

Note how the prayer describes what the sick person can expect from being anointed with consecrated oil. The Rite of Anointing generally expects the sick to "be freed from pain and illness," especially when the illness keeps the sick person from loving God, neighbor or himself. When we pray over a person who is in pain, such as those with rheumatoid arthritis, often the first sign of healing is that the pain decreases or disappears. Perhaps the Lord does this first because pain is usually non-redemptive, making it difficult for a person to focus beyond himself and reach out in love. Occasionally physical healing is total and immediate, but usually it requires time if the "mind and soul" are to be brought into wholeness also.

Larry, for example, had his arthritic arm healed immediately, but returned five times to a prayer group before his knee was free of arthritis. In sharing, he noted that "what I appreciated more than the arthritic healing was the group of people who prayed with me every week and became my first real friends. If Jesus had healed my arthritis all at once, I may not have come back, or even if I did come back, I doubt that I would know you in the same way." Sometimes physical healing is immediate, or the natural healing process is speeded up. Sometimes the healing takes place but natural damage remains, as when Carol's hearing returned despite nerve damage. The Lord knows best when and how to heal.

We should always expect prayer for healing to begin to heal the heart's fear, anger and guilt, as it did for Larry in his arthritic loneliness. Most emotional suffering is not redemptive but, like depression, chokes our power to love and to be at one with God, others and our deeper self. This healing is deepened the more we can listen to the sick person's struggles and enter into his breaking heart with the heart of Jesus. This process of inner healing of the hurtful emotions we describe simply in *Healing of Memories* and more thoroughly in *Healing Life's Hurts*.[2]

Healing through prayer heals more than the body and mind. When Jesus Christ is the focus of healing, we receive the ultimate healing, the experience of being unconditionally loved by Jesus. While working in emergency rooms we saw many people leave the hospital with healed bodies, only to return a month later on a drug overdose. At a level deeper than physical health, they had the gangrenous wound of being unloved. No pills or surgery can heal their broken spirit, but when Jesus Christ touches their wound, they become empowered to receive and give love. Those who are most alive are not necessarily those who are physically strongest, but those who feel loved and who communicate love the most. As Jesus' unconditional love touches us, the love invites us to love him and others and thus live life more fully.

Early Christians experienced so much fullness of life and healing from the oil blessed for the sick that they began to use and sell it as a magical potion needing no accompanying prayer. This led the Church to limit the use of sacramental oil to the clergy. But today oil can again be blessed nonsacramentally to use along with healing prayer for the sick. Just as lay people are invited to use holy water as an extension of baptismal water, so too, lay people are invited to use oil as an extension of the sacrament of the sick. The following quote from Fr. MacNutt's latest book, *The Power To Heal*, (Ave Maria Press, 1977) helps to explain this tradition.

> Many Catholic priests are not aware of this, but there is a blessing for oil which is for everyday healing use, and which people can then take home and use in praying for each other. There is no indication that this oil is limited to the sacrament of Anointing or to the bishop or priest (although its blessing is reserved to the bishop or priest).[3]

This prayer for the non-sacramental blessing of oil is found in the Appendix on pages 102–103.

In his blessing the priest transforms the ordinary substance of oil into a means of supernatural power to bring wholeness into the lives of the sick. He asks our loving Father to send the Holy Spirit upon the oil so that all who are anointed may be freed from pain and illness and made whole again in body, mind and soul.

Like most Christians reared in the Roman Catholic tradition, I (Barbara) accepted by faith the belief that the prayers said over water, salt, crucifixes, religious articles and oil, conferred special graces upon these items. However, after observing the reactions sacramentals evoke from people troubled by evil spirits, their power is readily apparent to me.

During one of our workshops in Latin America, Fathers Francis MacNutt and Paul Schaaf were praying over a man who had been involved in spiritualism. Each time holy oil touched his body, the man screamed as if burned by a branding iron, twisting and turning to avoid the anointing. Similar behavior occurred when he was sprinkled with holy water, but he became irrational when a consecrated host was brought into the room, even though the man had not been told it was present. I have noted this type of reaction to blessed substances many times since that day, deepening my appreciation for the priests' blessing prayers.

As in the early days of Christianity, the laity are again encouraged to use this blessed oil for all bodily ailments, whether it be a simple cut or a more serious sickness. Christians relied on spontaneous anointing prayers until 800 A.D., and Christians are once again invited to use the oil for healing with spontaneous prayers that arise from their hearts.

Unfortunately many people do not trust that their spontaneous heartfelt prayer is the prayer of Christ longing to heal with his infinite power. Yet prayers said with deep compassion can be more powerful than prayers by those with a more practiced gift of healing prayer.

Matt speaks of the many times a mother has brought a sick child to him and, as only a mother can, has hugged the child and asked Matt to pray for healing.

"But when I see that hug, I know that this mother can express Christ's love and intense longing for healing at a depth my prayer would never reach. So I often tell the mother that I will pray for the child because I know Jesus loves the child. I tell her that through our prayer Jesus once more wants to let a child climb on his lap, and that because she loves her child more than I do, her prayer, rather than mine, will be closer to Jesus' loving prayer.

"I ask her if she would mind praying the powerful prayer Jesus has placed in her heart while I silently pray with her, and when she is finished I will simply say whatever is in my heart.

"Far more happens when a mother prays from the intense pain and love in her heart than when I pray for her child. Not only does the child get well but the mother and child grow closer as the child hears and feels the depth of the mother's love."

The gift of healing is really the gift of love. To the degree we love as Jesus did, we will anoint and heal in his name and with his power. Blessing oil, which lay people may use in anointing the sick, should make us all aware of our particular gifts for healing those we can love uniquely.

—*Barbara*
—*Matt and Dennis*

Chapter 7
Prayer of Thanksgiving

On Thanksgiving Day both body and soul are nourished as we carve the roasted turkey and give thanks for the past year's blessings. We gather around the groaning table and try to pay attention not just to the steaming raisin dressing but also to the blessing before the meal.

During our last year's Thanksgiving feast, every person in our family was invited to mention one thing they were grateful for this past year. Four-year-old Tom couldn't remember anything, so he simply thanked God for "everything *next* year." Tom stretched us all to give deeper thanks since it is much easier to be grateful for past gifts than future gifts.

As Tom gave thanks for the future, so the Rite now calls on us to give praise to the Father, Son and Holy Spirit for the future healing that will come through the anointing. If it seems strange to thank God for healing before we receive it, we should consider the words of Jesus, "I tell you therefore, everything you ask and pray

for, believe that you have it already and it will be yours''
(Mk 11:24). Our faith leads us to expect that Jesus will
come as the Bread of Life at the Eucharist and we give
praise and thanks before we receive him. We should also
have as firm a belief leading us to praise and thank Jesus
in advance for his expected, certain healing. A Father
who sends his Son to live among us and heal us, a
Creator who presents us the Holy Spirit, the Consoler, is
ready to do anything that is best for us if we prepare our
hearts with praise and thanksgiving.

Praise itself can be very healing when it lifts us
out of ourselves and into the presence of the Lord.

Many charismatic prayer groups have discovered
the importance of having an extended period of praise
and thanksgiving at the beginning of the meeting in order
to focus on the ''goodness of God.'' Praise creates an
atmosphere which allows us to become so receptive to
the Lord's healing love that very little time needs to be
spent on intercessory prayer.

It's difficult to remain burdened by the problems
in our lives when we pause to consider the magnitude of
our Father's love for us. During our workshops, we have
noted an increase in the number of healings which occur
when the participants are willing to spend extended time
in thanksgiving prayer. Perhaps this is one of the reasons
why St. James prefaced his teaching about anointing the
sick by saying, ''Is anyone cheerful? Let him sing
praise'' (Jas 5:13).

—*Barbara*
—*Matt and Dennis*

Chapter 8
Anointing with Oil

Prayer heals not according to its length but according to its love, channeling the Lord's love and mercy given by his Spirit. The prayer that brought Lazarus back to life was simply one loving sentence, "Lord, he whom you love is sick" (Jn 11:4). Five-year-old Ricky continues to heal his family of flu, colds, backaches, with great child-like faith reminding Jesus, "Mommy's back hurts."

A first-grade teacher asks her pupils to pray for those who are absent and finds the first-graders' confident prayers produce major healings. Many charismatic prayer groups channel healing by simply praying in tongues with a heart full of the love of the Holy Spirit. The important thing is not the words or use of oil, but the channeling of God's healing love.

The oil should be applied as lovingly as Mary anointed Jesus' head at Bethany (Mk 14:3). Oil and this book's suggestions are merely a means for exercising

spiritual help, and are useless instruments without the
Holy Spirit's love in the user's heart.

We would expect a long, stately prayer to form
the climax of the new Rite, but, instead, find that the
priest prays only two sentences while anointing the sick
person on the forehead and hands:

> Through this holy anointing may the Lord in
> his love and mercy help you with the grace
> of the Holy Spirit. May the Lord who freed
> you from sin save you and raise you up.[1]

This prayer forms a fitting climax because it
briefly sums up the entire Rite. Since a priest prays the
sacramental prayer in the name of the community, this
prayer makes the Lord's love present in the entire community of the Church (introductory rite). It again reminds
us of the Lord's "mercy" in freeing the sick from sin
(penitential rite), and the Lord's mind and heart sent to
"love" the sick (scripture reading).

Finally, "May the Lord who freed you from sin
save you and raise you up" corresponds to the plea of the
litany, while the anointing of the hands and forehead with
oil brings both the healing power of touch and the healing
power of oil in order to confer health of mind, body and
soul.

When the Rite uses oil to ask for spiritual help,
usually only the forehead and hands are anointed, although "the number of anointings is to be adapted to the
occasion." Early Christians anointed any area of the
body affected by illness. The 11th century prayer of
Theodulf advised a minimum of 15 anointings, while the

Council of Trent directed that the five senses be anointed for purification. The new Rite no longer emphasizes anointing and purifying the senses, but offers to the sick the Lord's healing love and mercy through his Spirit. Though we usually don't anoint and purify the senses, we do find it helpful, when convenient, to anoint especially the part of the body in which the sickness or pain is centered.

Though the Rite allows for anointing various parts of the body, it stresses anointing the forehead and hands. The anointing of the forehead reminds us to ask the Spirit for peace of mind. Anointing the hands recalls that we are also praying for physical strength to flow out to the extremities so they can become the Lord's hands in loving service, embracing his cross redemptively until healing arrives. By the anointing we proclaim that the sick person is becoming *Christ* (meaning "the anointed one"), in the most loving way Jesus can come.

Oil is blessed and used, not just because Jesus sent out his Apostles to anoint (Mk 6:13), and because James says, "they must anoint the sick with oil," but because oil also symbolizes the way in which the Spirit is at work to heal the whole man—physically, mentally and spiritually.

Oil was used for physical healing in ancient times, e.g., the Good Samaritan poured oil into the wounds of the traveler to Jericho (Lk 10:34). Even today oil forms the base of most modern medicines, as well as the plastics used in surgical gloves and disposable syringes. The anointing with oil reminds us to pray over and use modern medicines; not to throw away our pills to "claim a healing" unless the doctor verifies the action.

The book of Sirach reminds us of the ancient wisdom, a wisdom even more true today with the advances of medicine:

> My son, when you are ill, do not be depressed, but pray to the Lord and he will heal you. Renounce your faults, keep your hands unsoiled, and cleanse your heart from all sin. Offer incense and a memorial of fine flour, and make as rich an offering as you can afford. Then let the doctor take over—the Lord created him, too—and do not let him leave you, for you need him. Sometimes success is in their hands, since they in turn will beseech the Lord to grant them the grace to relieve and to heal, that life may be saved. A man sins in the eyes of his Maker if he defies the doctor. (Sir 38:9-15)

Sirach's words "to pray to the Lord. . . .and then let the doctor take over" echo closely the plea of St. Caesarius of Arles (c. 525 A.D.) who healed many through prayer and anointing, yet continued to wish, "If at least they would look for health from ordinary medical care."[2] But prayer can also enrich "ordinary medical care" as it performs its daily tasks such as diagnosing illness or prescribing medicine. For instance, cancer specialist and noted author, Dr. Larry Samuels, finds that his days of highest accuracy with his cancer scanner are those days when he prays for guidance before seeing each patient.[3]

Doctors, nurses and patients can pray not only for help in the diagnosis, but also for the Lord to bless the medicine or surgery so it will heal faster. One nurse who prayed over her tray of medicine, reported that she needed to administer one-third the normal pain medication.

We must continue in the tradition of St. Basil who healed the sick both by prayer and by building the first hospital. Christianity differs from other world religions in its desire to bring God's healing through the medical profession.[4]

Oil calls us to expect physical healing as well as emotional healing of our fears, anger and guilt. The ancient Jewish law permitted anointings to occur during hopeful times of feasts, and to be omitted when a person desired to fast and mourn. (cf. Ruth 3:3; Mt 6:17). Esteemed guests were anointed, while hidden anger made Simon the Pharisee neglect to anoint Jesus (Lk 7:46). The anointing with oil is a sign that we expect to be filled with hope and become one with those around us.

Oil calls us to be spiritually healed in order to become one with Christ. It proclaims our identity with Jesus just as he prayed we would become one with him and with the Father. We have been anointed with health and with the Spirit in order to use that health in Christ's mission "to bring good news to the poor" (Is 61:1). We should expect what David experienced when anointed by Samuel, "From that day on the Spirit of the Lord rushed upon David" (I Sam 16:13).

—Matt and Dennis

As the priest anoints the sick person with oil, he is bringing comfort to a suffering body and conferring new life to a spirit. Because the oil has been blessed to convey wholeness, it is more than a light-colored fluid; it is a powerful means for carrying God's healing love.

More than once I've observed dramatic changes in a person's condition immediately following the anointing with oil. For instance, a small child, who was experiencing constant convulsive seizures, became relaxed and peaceful as she was blessed with holy oil. Another time a truck driver bleeding profusely from a deep laceration of his forehead was almost instantaneously healed as a modern-day good Samaritan anointed him with oil while they were awaiting the arrival of an ambulance. The emergency room physician did not even need to suture the wound because it had nearly disappeared.

This portion of the rite of Anointing emphasizes the effectiveness of holy oil for the restoration of our entire being. Most of us, at some time in our lives, have experienced the beneficial effects of soothing oil. It is beautiful to observe the contented expression on the face of an infant as his mother gently massages the sweet smelling liquid into his skin. Hospital patients consider it a special treat to receive a backrub accompanied by the application of an oil-base lotion. Most salves for itches, burns or scratches contain some form of oil reminding us of the universal use of this substance.

Matt and Dennis gave an example of a nurse who prayed over pain medication with interesting results. I would like to encourage everyone to pray over any type of medicine they are taking, asking the Lord to bless it and make it useful for healing. Most Christians would never partake of a meal without saying a blessing over the food, yet we fail to have the same consideration for the medicine we ingest. We should ask Jesus to remove any side effects from the drugs we take and infuse them with his healing power. I know of several persons who were completely protected from the adverse effects of cancer chemotherapy through the power of prayer which surrounded them during their treatments. They were certainly following the injunction of St. Paul, "Whatever you eat, whatever you drink, whatever you do at all, do it for the glory of God" (I Cor 10:31).

There is no conflict between medicine and healing prayer—both methods can work in partnership to bring wholeness to the individual. Our modern hospital system was founded by Christian women and men who recognized the necessity of treating the total person through every means available. In recent years there has been a renewal of spirituality among many members of the medical profession, prompting the formation of the Association of Christian Therapists in 1975.[5] This professional organization seeks to bring together all branches of medicine in order to explore the correlation between prayer and wholeness. There cannot be true healing unless the entire person is freely functioning in body, mind and spirit, a process which requires a lifetime of integration.

Many centuries ago, the philosopher Plato warned: "This is the great error of our day in the treatment of the human body, that physicians separate the soul from the body." In our modern scientific world we are just beginning to recognize the truth of that statement. Much evidence is being compiled in medical journals concerning psychosomatic illnesses (psyche-soul, soma-body), and the list grows longer every day. There is much we do not understand about the relationship between soul and body but, balancing the two is one of the purposes of this sacrament.

—Barbara

Chapter 9
Prayer after Anointing

Just as the sun has more warmth when focused to a pinpoint through a magnifying glass, so, too, the healing love of Jesus Christ seems to intensify when focused through specific prayer. After the general prayer for healing, the priest must select one of the following:

1) full health with no pain;

2) health coming through suffering;

3) health and patience for coping with the weakness of old age;

4) strength and hope of salvation for those in great danger; and,

5) strength, forgiveness and relief of pain for those about to die.

The priest prays both for healing and for strength to endure the suffering so the illness can be redemptive and growthful until total healing comes. Too often we pray either for healing or for the sick to have strength "to bear their cross of sickness," when the Lord wants to enable us to do both in the process of healing. Thus the purpose of the rite is not only to help the sick person "to bear his suffering bravely, but also to fight against it."[1]

Christ's healing can range from full health to the ultimate healing—healing of the body through death. How do we discern the way Jesus wants to heal this person? Rev. Tommy Tyson answers, "I give one ear to the sick person and the better ear to the Lord." Thus we listen to the sick person, listen to the Lord, and pray in the way the Holy Spirit leads. Some people seem to receive a "word from the Lord," or an image, helping them to focus their prayer on the specific way the Lord wants to work. However, Dennis notes that he finds it difficult to sort out the Lord's desires from his own human compassion.

"Rather than relying totally on my feelings, I find it helpful to simply ask the sick person after a few minutes of prayer; 'What are you experiencing?' His answer helps me to discover how the Lord appears to be working in order to blend my prayer with the will of the Father.

"An elderly woman with back problems told me through tears that she had just lost her husband. I prayed then, not for the physical healing of her back, but for inner healing of her grief. As the grief was unloaded through tears, the love of Jesus poured into her heart and her back pain began to disappear."

Recently a woman with her arm in a sling asked for prayers. After a few minutes Matt asked what she was experiencing. "She felt a tingling and warmth in her toes, so I shifted from her arm to praying for her chronic hammer toes which rapidly began to spread out. Healing seems to occur more frequently when, after listening to the person, we ask the Lord how to pray, pray a while, and then discern further by simply asking the person what he is experiencing. In this way we are calling upon all the resources available to us as we try to discover the direction of our prayers.''

—*Matt and Dennis*

The prayer after anointing of the Rite requires the priest to discern the proper way to pray for the person who is ill. It reminds us of the necessity for seeking God's guidance as we intercede for those who are in need.

The epistle of James states very clearly, "Why you don't have what you want is because you don't pray for it; and when you do pray and don't get it, it is because you have not prayed properly, you have prayed for something to indulge your own desires" (Jas 4:3). This scripture is exhorting us to make our requests specifically known to the Lord and, then, to ascertain his will in the situation.

My work in the healing ministry has convinced me of the important role the prayer for guidance plays. We can expend much energy peititioning the Lord for things which would not be beneficial for ourselves or for others. It becomes necessary to approach every situation with the prayer, "Lord, how should I pray for this person?", puting aside our own preconceived ideas and desires.

During a workshop in Illinois, I was asked to pray with a man who was suffering from the effects of a massive coronary condition. For many weeks he had been lying in the coronary care unit while a constant stream of people prayed over him for healing. Before going to the hospital, I prayed for guidance, asking the Lord to show me the best way to minister to this man. It seemed as if the Holy Spirit was instructing me to pray for a healing of the relationship between this man and his wife. During the years I've learned to rely on these internal promptings as I've tested the accuracy of the "still, small voice" within myself. Therefore, I prayed with the man, asking Jesus to bring his marriage into order and remove the barriers between husband and wife. After the prayer, he appeared to be resting quietly so I went home.

At a prayer meeting many weeks later, he told the group that he could feel his body starting to be healed as he entered into the prayer for his marriage. The moment he told the Lord that he was willing to be reunited with his spouse, his physical condition began to improve. Following his discharge from the hospital, the couple received marriage counseling which greatly aided their relationship.

The Holy Spirit will always guide us to pray for wholeness in a person's life, but we need to be open to the possibility that total health might only be accomplished in the next life. A group of people interceding for a seriously ill friend will often receive scripture and prophesy confirming that the Lord wills to heal this person. If he should die, they then become upset and confused over the apparent contradiction, forgetting that eternal life with our Lord is the ultimate healing we are all longing to attain. The Lord always wills to heal a person, but we may need to pray for further guidance before we can begin to understand his messages.

God alone can see the total picture of our lives and, as we turn to him for wisdom, he will light the path before us, enabling us to see his perfect way.

—Barbara

Chapter 10
The Lord's Prayer

We can be so familiar with the Our Father that we sometimes fail to pay attention to the meaning of this glorious prayer. The priest intones the first two words and we spontaneously recite the entire prayer.

The Lord's prayer is placed in the Rite of Anointing not only as a preparation for Communion, but also to remind us that we are interceding for all our Father's sick children. We address God as a heavenly Father who desires wholeness for his sick child as much as a human father does. "If you, then, who are evil, know how to give your children what is good, how much more will your Father in heaven give good things to those who ask him!" (Mt. 7:11). To the degree we channel the love of our Father in heaven to the sick, we heal the sick. We ask that our Father's name be hallowed by the healing, just as Jesus asked for the blind to see so his Father might be glorified.

We are not asking just for health—but health which will enable us to be placed lovingly in the Father's service so his kingdom might come *now* upon the earth. When praying that his will be done "on earth as it is in heaven," we are asking to receive at this moment the fullness of life. We are prone to use this portion of the prayer out of context when we stress the phrase, "your will be done," at the end of our prayers, without finishing the entire sentence. Expressing the whole thought places the emphasis on our expectancy that the heavenly kingdom, where there is no sickness, sorrow or death, will gradually come upon this earth.

For his kingdom to come, we ask to receive his strength through the direct touch of his power and, also, through the daily bread he provides, including medicine, nutritious food and doctor's care. The Father will use every means available in order to bring us into wholeness.

The burgeoning field of psychosomatic medicine reinforces the request to receive and give forgiveness of trespasses so we can be released from any anger or guilt which causes or prolongs our illness. We don't wait until we "feel" loving towards another, but we decide to cease harboring resentment, hurt feelings or hatred. This act of our will opens the door of our spirit to enable the Lord to begin to bless our lives.

The prayer finishes with a request to be protected from temptation and from all future evil leading to illness. This portion of the Our Father is actually a prayer for deliverance. When we say, "save us from the evil one," we are literally asking the Lord to protect us from the devil and all his subtle attacks. It has been said that Jesus only comes in when he is invited, but Satan never waits to be asked. He is always attempting to lead God's people astray. Jesus, too, had several encounters with the evil one, but his Father never failed to shield him from harm.

One of Satan's attacks is to make healing sound too complicated, discouraging us before we begin. However, we needn't be confused by all the facets of the Rite of Anointing if we but recall the simplicity of the Lord's prayer. It summarizes all that is necessary in approaching our loving Father.

—Barbara
—Matt and Dennis

Chapter 11
Communion

Communion is not just the act of becoming one with the Lord's Body in bread, but of becoming one with the Lord's Body in people. We will be healthier to the degree that we see Jesus in the people who are continually hurting us. When the Eucharist becomes a commitment to love our enemy with the love of Christ, then another level of healing begins. If Eucharist doesn't make us one with others, then it is hypocrisy which hurts rather than heals. That's why St. Paul could tell the Corinthians who received the Eucharist, yet refused to share their food: "Everyone is to recollect himself before eating this bread and drinking this cup; because a person who eats and drinks without recognizing the Body is eating and drinking his own condemnation. In fact, that is why many of you are weak and ill and some of you have died" (1 Cor 11:28-30). The Eucharist brings illness or health, depending on whether we receive just bread or the whole Christ present in his members.

Throughout history Christians have experienced health coming through the Eucharist. The earliest written rites, such as *Bishop Serapion's Prayer Book* (IV, 7) and the *Apostolic Constitutions* (VIII, 29) of Hippolytus, provide special prayers at the Eucharist for blessing oil, bread or even water to be used for healing the sick. St. Caesarius (502–542) also connects health with the Eucharist when he advises, "Come to Church, anoint yourselves with blessed oil, receive the Eucharist of Christ. If you do this, you will receive health not only for the body but also for the soul."[1]

Even today the oils for the Rite of Anointing the sick are blessed on Holy Thursday, the day dedicated to the institution of the Eucharist at the Last Supper. Each day the priest, before Communion, prays silently for "health of mind and body," then joins the people in praying the centurion's prayer for healing, "Lord, I am not worthy to receive you but only say the Word and I shall be healed." Healing is our last request before receiving the body and blood of Christ.

The reports of healing through receiving the Body and Blood of Christ in the Eucharist are as numerous as the pages of Christian history. The reports vary in their fact and fiction, but enough physical healing occurred that St. Caesarius (502–542 A.D.) and later St. Elygius (600 A.D.) were successful in having the sick reject their amulets and healing magic and receive the Eucharist and be anointed with oil.[2] Superstitious people switched from magic to the Eucharist, not because of wild healing stories or a theology of Eucharistic healing, but because it worked! The earliest recorded rites for the sick, such as the Carolingian ritual, all include the Eucharist. If the sick were not healed immediately, prayers were to be repeated and the Eucharist to be received for seven days.

Today, too, the Eucharist brings physical healing when received in expectation of healing, with an openness to the whole body of Christ. Gifted persons like Fr. Francis MacNutt find the best time for healing is right after a person has received the Eucharist and is resting in the healing power and love of Jesus Christ. This is likewise the experience of people who jam Our Lady of Mercy parish in Hicksville, New York, every First Friday of the month.[3] Because they have experienced the power of that Eucharist to heal everything from sore throats to cancer, they even overflow into the basement where they can only listen to the Mass upstairs.

While working as hospital chaplains, we too saw the Eucharist physically heal in many dramatic ways, such as sudden positive changes recorded on heart monitors, rapid drops in temperature from 101.8 to 98.8, blood pressures spontaneously changing 20 points, and the most common—healing accelerated so a patient recovers and goes home in half the expected time.

While sacramental churches such as Our Lady of Mercy discover the power of Jesus' Body and Blood present in the Eucharist, the nonsacramental churches are rediscovering the power in the blood of Jesus. Those in Pentecostal or Assembly of God churches petition the blood of Jesus to drive out the presence of evil and to bring healing. But even receiving the Eucharist or petitioning to be filled with the blood of Jesus can degenerate into a magical formula for healing.

Healing happens to the degree we meet Jesus, give him thanks for whatever healing has begun, and rest in his love and power within us. We can invite the Lord to come within us (spiritual communion) and transform our body cell by cell into his body. Often it is helpful to imagine the Lord's healing power like light emanating from the Eucharist living within us and warming the area of the body that needs healing.

"Eucharist" means "giving thanks" and the more we give thanks for past and present healing, the more the Lord makes whole the area of the body that needs healing. When we lead a Eucharist for healing, we spend most of the time thanking the Lord for his gifts and past healing, and then finally intercede for present needs. Agnes Sanford, who is one of the most respected and wise teachers of healing prayer, emphasizes strongly the need to finish healing prayer by giving thanks for healing that has already started.[4] The Eucharist heals not only by receiving Jesus in bread, but by also "giving thanks" for all he is accomplishing through this sacrament.

—Matt and Dennis

The celebration of Mass is a healing service, and the reception of the Lord's Body is the most powerful means granted to us for obtaining wholeness in body, mind and spirit. Jesus is present in the Eucharist in his resurrected person, filled with life and desiring to transfer this life into us. If we believe in this truth, we will be the healthiest of people.

Jesus told us, "whoever eats me will draw life from me" (Jn 6:57), as he encouraged us to receive his Body in order to become complete. As we approach the altar for Communion, we should be considering any specific areas within us which need healing, and appropriate the power of Jesus to make up for our imperfections. As far as we know, our Lord was never physically ill, nor did he suffer from emotional problems. Therefore, when we accept his Body into ours, we can expect greater wholeness.

The woman with a hemorrhage (Mt 9:20) understood this principle when she reached out her hand saying, "If I can only touch his cloak, I shall be well again." Her trust in the Lord's ability to cure her affliction brought new life into her body.

When we receive Jesus in the Eucharist, we are in even more intimate contact with his divine presence than this suffering woman. We are being permitted to partake of the total risen nature of Jesus Christ, not with our fingertips but our whole being. The healer abides within us in a magnificent way, bringing his light into the darkness of physical, emotional or spiritual needs.

During one of our workshops for nurses, Mary O'Keefe from Baldwin, New York, shared this story:

> "Nine years ago I was diagnosed as having acute rheumatoid arthritis and was placed on cortisone and arthritis medication. During the next seven years, I experienced varying degrees of swelling, pain, discomfort and deformity in several different areas of my body. I was never able to be without some type of medication.

> "Two years ago I attended a Mass emphasizing 'Healing through the Eucharist.' Even though I had been involved in the Charismatic Renewal for one year, I had been afraid to ask for healing of my arthritis. That evening I *did* ask Jesus to heal me as I received him in Communion. Within a few weeks I noticed that my symptoms had disappeared, I was able

to discontinue all medication and have had no recurrence.

"Now I receive the Eucharist in thanksgiving for my continued good health."

This example is one of hundreds I have heard from Christians who seriously consider the reality of God's healing love through the reception of Holy Communion. We can similarly call upon this grace to assist us with emotional difficulties, remembering that the mind of Christ is also resident in the sacrament.

A young friend of mine was in great need of inner healing for memories from his early childhood. His parents were killed in an airplane crash and he had been sent to live with various relatives, some of whom treated him cruelly. He asked me to pray with him but there always seemed to be last minute conflicts blocking our meeting.

One morning, while he was at Mass, he suddenly realized that Jesus, present in the Eucharist, was perfectly able to touch his unconscious mind and relieve him of the burdens he carried. As he received the Body of Christ, he asked Jesus to go back into his childhood and free the little boy who felt so rejected and alone. In his imagination he pictured the Lord holding the child in his strong arms in order to protect him from harm. He experienced years of fear and tension being washed away as he thanked Jesus for giving him new life. This same life is readily available to all of us, each time we celebrate the Eucharist.

The Rite of Anointing offers the sick person the gift of the Body of Christ along with the other graces resident in the sacrament. The Church provides us with every opportunity to obtain wholeness.

—Barbara

Chapter 12
Blessing

The rite of the sick closes with one of two blessings for continued healing and protection from harm. The blessing asks that God's help may continue beyond our healing prayer together. Most healings are not immediate, but, rather, "process" healings that begin or continue days after the healing prayer. Even Jesus did not heal a certain blind man immediately, but had to pray again that the "walking trees" he saw would be focused into men (Mk 8:22–25).

The oldest written healing rite, Alcuin's Carolingian Order, advises that the entire rite be repeated daily for seven days.[1] Today's rite for the sick also advises that the ritual be repeated "if the sick person recovers after anointing, or if during the same illness the danger becomes more serious."[2] Since a person always gets at least a little better or worse, repeating the sacrament's healing prayer is encouraged.

Today we are beginning to see the wisdom of

repeating the healing prayer. Fr. Francis MacNutt, with his extraordinary gift of praying for physical healing, claims that only 25% seem to be healed immediately, another 50% are healed gradually if they continue to pray for healing, and 25% seem not to be physically healed. Most are healed gradually if prayer is continued over days and months.

Unfortunately, this wisdom of continual prayer for healing is not as widely known as the practice of telling the sick to "claim their healing." We even saw a group try to get a man with a broken leg to walk on his leg and claim that it was healed. That might be valid if he is in the 25% that are immediately healed but, should he be among the other 75%, he could sustain a compound fracture. Somehow people feel that if they claim their healing, they are showing more faith and more will be done. Actually, it takes more faith to claim only as much as God has really healed, believe that his way and time are more loving than our desires, and then to pray daily for further healing. Claiming healing that hasn't happened can ultimately undermine the person's faith in healing prayer, hurt him as he avoids the doctors and medication he needs, or prevent him from continuing soaking prayer that might bring greater wholeness. It's best to claim only what the Lord has done and what the doctor verifies.

As a general rule, the more serious and chronic the illness, the longer it takes continued soaking prayer for healing. What takes longer for medicine to heal generally takes longer for healing prayer, perhaps because prayer most often accelerates the natural process of healing. Accidental cuts usually need less prayer than chronic rheumatoid arthritis.

A close friend has been praying for several months with a woman who has an immobilized hand half its regular size. With weekly soaking prayer, sensation returned, then movement, then the fingers straightened slowly and the hand started to fill out. None of this would have happened if she had just prayed once. If something begins to happen, such as release from pain, it's usually a sign the Lord will do more healing through soaking prayer.

Perhaps healing prayer by now sounds too complicated. It is as easy and as complex as loving. Lovers will daily find new ways to express their feelings for one another. Likewise, if we love the sick with Christ's love, we will be led to pray in many ways not mentioned in this book. Healing the sick means prayerfully loving the sick as Jesus does. One mother who understands the Lord's heart and prays powerfully for healing revealed her secret: I love; I listen; I hug; I pray.

—*Matt and Dennis*

The Rite of Anointing concludes with a blessing by the priest which reads, in part: "May God the Father bless you; may God the Son heal you; may God the Holy Spirit enlighten you."

We are invoking the Trinity and enlisting all assistance in the completion of our prayer for healing, as we thank the Lord for the things he has already accomplished and praise him for what is still to come.

Matt and Dennis have already discussed the fact that healing is a process requiring us to continue seeking wholeness through all the means available to us. Many times we have witnessed spontaneous healings, sometimes of serious, chronic ailments, and it has filled our hearts with joy to see these manifestations of God's power.

However, we have not been oblivious to the sufferings of those who are not immediately set free. Kathryn Kuhlman summed it up when she said: ''The first question I will ask the Lord when I get to heaven is, 'Why weren't they all healed?' '' She has undoubtedly received the answer, while we must still walk by faith through the mysterious ways of God.

Although I don't know why everyone isn't healed, I do know we have been commanded to seek the wholeness which will enable us to approach God and our neighbors in an ever deeper commitment of love. Anything which impedes our ability to love and be loved, is not in the will of God. If my physical condition is causing me to become so self-centered that I can no longer lovingly care for my family, it needs to be healed. If my mind is so confused I am no longer able to make rational decisions, I can be very certain that Jesus wants to set me free.

The problem arises when we attempt to make God into our image and likeness instead of vice versa. His timetable for answered prayer may not be in accordance with ours and, therefore, we feel rejected and angry when things don't live up to our expectations. However, if we could see the situation with the eyes of the Lord, we would realize the complexity of the entire process.

Jesus is not only healing our physical symptoms, but also transforming the old thought patterns and bad habits which caused us to be sick in the first place. Even those who have been spontaneously freed from serious illnesses usually are led through a period of spiritual cleansing where they are confronted with any disorder in their lives.

Jesus wants to bring abundant life to every portion of our being. If we would patiently trust in his infinite goodness as we ask for his healing love to become manifested, the Kingdom of God would soon be realized.

—Barbara

Epilogue
Prayer for Healing

The Rite of Anointing presents us with a means of experiencing the compassion and love of our heavenly Father. The steps in the sacrament are meant to lead us into an ever deepening awareness of his presence in our lives as we turn to the source of all life. God is not an abstract Deity but a Creator who desires to be intimately involved in every aspect of our search for wholeness.

The Father patiently waits to be invited into this process, since he never disregards our free will, but gives us the freedom to accept or reject the graces provided for us. Therefore, the first requirement for receiving the Lord's healing love is to ask him to assume dominion over our entire being. We need to recognize our futile attempts to earn salvation through self-effort and return to the foot of the cross where the ransom was paid once and for all.

Perhaps you have never considered the importance of inviting Jesus Christ into your life. He is already aware of your needs and is longing to draw you closer to himself, but the door only opens from your side . . .

> Father, I realize that there are many areas in my life where I need your healing touch. I have hesitated to ask for healing for a variety of reasons, but I come before you today, feeling somewhat like one half-dead on an abandoned roadside. I ask you, Father, to send Jesus down that roadway to care for me (Lk 10:29–37).

> Jesus, you come upon me with my bruises and open wounds. As you stop, your gaze sees all the events that caused those wounds and made me feel half-dead. As I feel your hand touching and examining each wound, I thank you that you are not like the priest and Levite, but that you love me just the way I am.

> Your healing touch invites me to open my squinting eyes. I feel your warm healing light penetrating through my eyes, filling my entire self, and infusing me with new life. Wherever I've been filled with darkness and despair, let your light penetrate those areas until I see through your eyes. (Pause and bask in Jesus' healing light.)

> As your interior warmth allows my whole body to become like wax ready to be reshaped, I give you all those parts of my body which have suffered from illness, especially any that are right now in pain. Jesus, you know what it is like to endure pain; please anoint my body with your soothing oil, quiet the nerve endings and allow me to rest in comfort.

> And as I begin to rest in comfort, let me focus my attention on one physically wounded part

of my body. Let me allow you to be the Good Samaritan as I feel the soothing of your oil and the firmness of your bandage. Let me see how you reshape and make that part of my body new, just as you and your Father fashioned me with such exacting precision at the moment of my conception. (Pause and watch Jesus making your body new in the most loving way.)

And Jesus, when you were the good Samaritan, you made provisions with the innkeeper to continue the medical care and healing you had started. Bless those also who care for me when I am ill. Please give your gift of wisdom to my physician that he may be guided by your Holy Spirit in all he does. Bless too my medication and my nurses so that their hands will become your hands as they touch me.

Most of all, I ask you to fill my heart with your peace and love as a sure sign of your presence in me. As your presence touches my body and spirit in the most loving way, may we become more intimate so that at my death we will greet each other as old friends rather than as new acquaintances.

Sometimes we will be too weak or tired to pray like this. At such times healing prayer may be simply looking at a crucifix and repeating "Father" as Jesus did long ago upon his cross on Calvary and as Jesus longs to do now upon His cross within us. We don't even need words, but can simply breathe in the Father's love and strength and breathe out the tension and discouragement, until our body feels relaxed and surrendered part by part. We can start with the wrinkles in the forehead and with each inhalation fill the forehead with the Father's love, and with each exhalation drain out the tension until the forehead feels relaxed and its cares are surrendered to the Father's hands. We can continue this part by part down the eyes, face, jaw, neck and on down the body until reaching the toes and wiggling them as does a child fondled by his father's loving hand. We have a Father who wants to heal us in his time and much more than any father wants his child healed.

> Is there a man among you who would hand his son a stone when he asked for bread? Or would hand him a snake when he asked for a fish? If you, then, who are evil, know how to give your children what is good, how much more will your Father in heaven give good things to those who ask him! (Mt 7:9-11).

—Barbara
—Matt and Dennis

Appendices
Rite of Anointing a Sick Person

1. INTRODUCTORY RITE

Wearing the appropriate vestments, the priest approaches the sick person and greets him (her) and the others present in a friendly manner. He may use this greeting:

The peace of the Lord be with you.

According to the circumstances, the priest may sprinkle the sick person and the room with holy water, saying the following words or those given in a particular ritual:

**Let this water call to mind
your baptismal sharing
in Christ's redeeming passion and
resurrection.**

Then he addresses those present in these or similar words:

**Dear brothers and sisters,
we have come together in the name of our Lord**

Jesus Christ, who restored the sick to health,
and who himself suffered so much for our
sake. He is present among us as we recall the
words of the Apostle James: "Is there anyone
sick among you? Let him call for the elders of
the Church, and let them pray over him and
anoint him in the name of the Lord. This
prayer, made in faith, will save the sick man.
The Lord will restore his health, and if he has
committed any sins, they will be forgiven."

Let us entrust our sick brother (sister) N. to
the grace and power of Jesus Christ, that the
Lord may ease his (her) suffering and grant
him (her) health and salvation.

2. PENITENTIAL RITE

If there is no sacramental confession, the penitential rite then follows.

My brothers and sisters, to prepare ourselves
for this holy anointing, let us call to mind
our sins.

After a brief silence, all say:

I confess to almighty God,
and to you, my brothers and sisters,
that I have sinned through my own fault
in my thoughts and in my words,
in what I have done,
and in what I have failed to do;
and I ask blessed Mary, ever Virgin,
all the angels and saints,
and you, my brothers and sisters,
to pray for me to the Lord our God.

The priest concludes:

> **May almighty God have mercy on us,**
> **forgive us our sins,**
> **and bring us to everlasting life.**

> R. Amen.

3. READING FROM SCRIPTURE

Then a brief text from scripture is read by one of those present or by the priest.

> **Brothers and sisters, listen to the words of the Gospel according to John.**

> **Truly, truly, I say to you, he who believes in me will also do the works that I do: and greater works than these will he do, because I go to the Father. Whatever you ask in my name, I will do it, that the Father may be glorified in the Son. If you ask anything in my name, I will do it (Jn 14:12–14).**

4. LITANY

> **My brothers and sisters, with faith let us ask the Lord to hear our prayers for our brother (sister) N.**

> **Lord, through this holy anointing, come and comfort N. with your love and mercy.**

> R. Lord, hear our prayer.

> **Free N. from all harm.**

> R. Lord, hear our prayer.

> **Relieve the suffering of all the sick (here present).**

R. Lord, hear our prayer.

Assist all those dedicated to the care of the sick.

R. Lord, hear our prayer.

Free N. from sin and all temptation.

R. Lord, hear our prayer.

Give life and health to our brother (sister) N., on whom we lay our hands in your name.

R. Lord, hear our prayer.

5. LAYING ON OF HANDS

The priest then lays his hands on the head of the sick person in silence.

6. BLESSING OF OIL

Let us pray.
Lord God, loving Father,
you bring healing to the sick
through your Son Jesus Christ.
Hear us as we pray to you in faith,
and send the Holy Spirit, man's Helper and
 Friend,
upon this oil, which nature has provided
to serve the needs of men.
May your blessing +
come upon all who are anointed with this oil,
that they may be freed from pain and illness
and made well again in body, mind and soul.
Father, may this oil be blessed for our use
in the name of our Lord Jesus Christ
who lives and reigns with you for ever and
 ever.

R. Amen.

7. PRAYER OF THANKSGIVING

If the oil is already blessed, the priest says the prayer of thanksgiving over it:

Praise to you, almighty God and Father.
You sent your Son to live among us and bring us salvation.
R. Blessed be God.
Praise to you, Lord, Jesus Christ,
the Father's only Son.
You humbled yourself to share in our humanity,
and you desired to cure all our illnesses.
R. Blessed be God.
Praise to you, God the Holy Spirit, the Consoler.
You heal our sickness with your mighty power.
R. Blessed be God.
Lord God,
with faith in you
our brother (sister)
will be anointed with this holy oil.
Ease his (her) sufferings and strengthen him (her) in his (her) weakness.
We ask this through Christ our Lord.
R. Amen.

8. ANOINTING

Then the priest takes the oil and anoints the sick person on the forehead and the hands, saying once:

Through this holy anointing
may the Lord in his love and mercy help you
with the grace of the Holy Spirit.

R. Amen.

**May the Lord who freed you from sin
save and raise you up.**
R. Amen.

9. PRAYER AFTER ANOINTING

Afterwards the priest says one of the following prayers:

Let us pray.

A) *For full health with no pain*
**Lord Jesus Christ, our Redeemer,
by the power of the Holy Spirit
ease the sufferings of our sick brother (sister)
and make him (her) well again in mind and
    body.
In your loving kindness forgive his (her) sins
and grant him (her) full health
so that he (she) may be restored to your ser-
    vice.
You are Lord for ever and ever.**

R. Amen.

B) *For health coming through suffering*
**Lord Jesus Christ,
you shared in our human nature
to heal the sick and save all mankind.
Mercifully listen to our prayers
for the physical and spiritual health of our sick
    brother (sister)
whom we have anointed in your name.
May your protection console him (her)
and your strength make him (her) well again.
[Help him (her) find hope in suffering,**

for you have given him (her) a share in your
   passion.]
You are Lord for ever and ever.

R. Amen.

C) *When the illness is the result of advanced age*
Lord,
look kindly on our brother (sister)
who has grown weak under the burden of his
   (her) years.
In this holy anointing
he (she) asks for the grace of health in body
   and soul.
By the power of your Holy Spirit,
make him (her) firm in faith and sure in hope,
so that his (her) cheerful patience
may reveal your love for us.
We ask this through Christ our Lord.

R. Amen.

D) *When the sick person is in great danger*
Lord Jesus Christ,
you took our weakness on yourself
and bore our sufferings in your passion and
   death.
Hear this prayer for our suffering brother (sister) N.
You are his (her) redeemer:
strengthen his (her) hope for salvation
and in your kindness sustain him (her)
in body and soul.
You live and reign for ever and ever.

R. Amen.

E) *For those about to die*

Lord God, loving Father,
you are the source of all goodness and love,
and you never refuse forgiveness
to those who are sorry for their sins.
Have mercy on your son (daughter) N.,
who is about to return to you.
May this holy anointing
and our prayers made in faith assist him (her):
relieve his (her) pain, in body and soul,
forgive all his (her) sins,
and strengthen him (her) with your loving pro-
    tection.
We ask this, Father, through your Son Jesus
    Christ,
who conquered death
and opened for us the way to eternal life,
and who lives and reigns for ever and ever.

R. Amen.

10. LORD'S PRAYER

Now let us pray to God as our Lord Jesus
    Christ taught us.
All: Our Father, ...

11. COMMUNION

This is the Lamb of God
who takes away the sins of the world.
Happy are those who are called to his supper.
R. Lord, I am not worthy to receive you,
but only say the word and I shall be healed.

The body of Christ (or: the blood of Christ.)

R. Amen.

After a period of silence, the priest concludes with:

Let us pray.
God our Father, almighty and eternal,
we confidently call upon you,
that the body (and blood) of Christ
which our brother (sister) has received
may bring him (her)
lasting health in mind and body.
We ask this through Christ our Lord.

R. Amen.

12. BLESSING

May God the Father bless you.
R. Amen.
May God the Son heal you.
R. Amen.
May God the Holy Spirit enlighten you.
R. Amen.
May God protect you from harm
and grant you salvation.
R. Amen.
May he shine on your heart
and lead you to eternal life.
R. Amen.
[And may almighty God,
the Father, and the Son, + and the Holy Spirit,
bless you all.]
R. Amen.

Blessing of Oil, For Use By Laity.*

Our help is in the name of the Lord,
R. Who made heaven and earth.

EXORCISM

God's creature, oil,

I cast out the demon from you by God the
Father almighty +

who made heaven and earth and sea and all
that they contain.

Let the adversary's power, the devil's legions,
and all Satan's attacks and machinations

be dispelled and driven afar from this creature, oil.

Let it bring health in body and mind to all who
use it,

in the name of God + the Father almighty,

and of our Lord Jesus Christ + his Son,

and of the Holy Spirit + the Advocate,

as well as in the love of the same Jesus Christ
our Lord,

who is coming to judge both the living and the
dead

and the world by fire.

R. Amen.

---

*The Roman Ritual, transl. by Philip Weller (Milwaukee: Bruce, 1964), p. 573.

Lord, heed my prayer.
R. And let my cry be heard by you.
The Lord be with you.
R. And also with you.

Let us pray.
Lord God almighty,
before whom the hosts of angels stand in awe
and whose heavenly service we acknowledge,
may it please you to regard favorably
and to bless and hallow this creature, oil,
which by your power has been pressed from
the juice of olives.
You have ordained it for anointing the sick, so
that,
when they are made well, they may give thanks
to you,
the living and true God.
Grant, we pray, that those who use this oil,
which we are blessing + in your name,
may be delivered from all suffering, all infir-
mity,
and all wiles of the enemy.
Let it be a means of averting any kind of ad-
versity from man,
made in your image and redeemed by the pre-
cious blood of your Son,
so that he may never again suffer the sting of
the ancient serpent,
through Christ our Lord.
R. Amen.

The oil is sprinkled with holy water.

Footnotes

Introduction

1. Barbara Shlemon, *Healing Prayer* (Notre Dame: Ave Maria Press, 1976).

Prologue

1. Much of the historical material in this book comes from a doctoral dissertation "Relationship Between the Sacrament of Anointing the Sick and the Charism of Healing Within the Catholic Charismatic Renewal." Louis Rogge, O.Carm., is currently writing this dissertation for Union Theological Seminary. Unless otherwise indicated, the historical material for this text comes from Louis Rogge and four other sources: 1. Morton Kelsey, *Healing and Christianity* (New York: Harper & Row, 1973). 2. Placid Murray, O.S.B., "The Liturgical History of Extreme Unction," in *The Furrow*, XI (1960), 572–593, citing Antoine Chavasse, *Etude II* (unpublished). 3. Paul F. Palmer, S.J., ed., *Sacraments and Forgiveness: History and Doctrinal Development of Penance, Extreme Unction and Indulgences*, Vol 2 of *Source of Christian Theology* (Westminster, Maryland: The Newman Press, 1959). 4. Bernhard Poschmann, S.J., *Penance and Anointing of the Sick*, tr. Francis Courteney (N.Y.: Herder, 1964).

Chapter 1

1. Henry James Coleridge, *Life and Letters of Francis Xavier* (London: Burns & Oates, 1874), 154–155.

2. Innocent I, *Epistolae et Decreta* 25,8.

3. Louis P. Rogge, O.Carm., "The Anointing of the Sick in Historical Perspective," *Linacre Quarterly,* 42:3 (August, 1975), 205–214.

4. Paul F. Palmer, S.J. "Who Can Anoint the Sick?" *Worship* 48:2 (February, 1974), 84–85.

5. *Rite of Anointing and Pastoral Care of the Sick* (N.Y.: Pueblo, 1974), 26. Will be referred to as *Rite of Anointing*.

6. *Ibid.,* 23.

7. *Ibid.,* 26.

8. *Ibid.,* 51.

9. Bishops' Committee on the Liturgy, *Study Text II: Anointing and Pastoral Care of the Sick: Commentary on the Rite for the Anointing and Pastoral Care of the Sick* (Washington: United States Catholic Conference, 1973), 22.

10. *Rite of Anointing,* 16.

11. Francis MacNutt, O.P., *The Power to Heal* (Notre Dame: Ave Maria Press, 1977), 47. Besides this book, Francis MacNutt's book, *Healing* (Notre Dame: Ave Maria Press, 1974) gives valuable information about why and how to pray for physical healing.

Chapter 2

1. *Rite of Anointing,* 50.

2. For a treatment of sacramental confession as healing see Michael Scanlan, T.O.R., *The Power in Penance* (Notre Dame: Ave Maria Press, 1972).

3. W.B. Cannon, "The Emergency Functions of the Adrenal Medulla in Pain and Major Emotions," *American Journal of Physiology,* 33 (1914), 356.

4. Meyer Friedman and Ray Rosenman, *Type-A Behavior and Your Heart* (Greenwich, Conn.: Fawcett, 1974).

5. For the relationship of emotional and physical components of various illnesses, see: David Graham, "Psychosomatic Medicine," in *Handbook of Psychophysiology,* ed. by Greenfield, Norman, and Sternbach (N.Y.: Holt, Rinehart and Winston, 1972), 839–924.

6. Hans Selye, *The Stress of Life* (N.Y.: McGraw-Hill, 1956).

Chapter 3

1. For a basic treatment of healing through active imagination,

cf. Ruth Stapleton, *The Gift of Inner Healing* (Waco, Texas: Word, 1976) and *The Experience of Inner Healing* (Waco, Texas: Word, 1977). Also cf. Morton Kelsey, *The Other Side of Silence* (N.Y.: Paulist, 1976) for the importance of imagination in prayer.

2. O. Carl Simonton and Stephanie S. Simonton, "Belief Systems and Management of Malignancy," *Journal of Transpersonal Psychology,* VII:1 (1975), 29–47.

Chapter 5

1. Irenaeus, *Contra Haeresis* II:32,4–5.

2. Ronald Sullivan, "Hospitals Introducing a Therapy Resembling 'Laying On of Hands,'" *New York Times* (New York: Nov 6, 1977).

3. Godfrey Diekmann, O.S.B., "The Laying on of Hands: The Basic Sacramental Rite," The Catholic Theological Society of America, *Proceedings of the Twenty-Ninth Annual Convention* (Chicago: 1974), 340.

Chapter 6

1. Probably A.D. 197; cf. Cyril Richardson, "The Date and Setting of the Apostolic Tradition of Hippolytus: A Preliminary Essay," *Anglican Theological Review* 30 (1948), 39,41.

2. Matthew and Dennis Linn, S.J., *Healing of Memories* (N.Y.: Paulist, 1974); idem, *Healing Life's Hurts* (N.Y.: Paulist, 1978). For a treatment of emotional healing through prayer.

3. Francis MacNutt, O.P., *Power to Heal, op.cit.,* 247–48.

Chapter 8

1. *Rite of Anointing and Pastoral Care of the Sick,* (N.Y.: Catholic Book Publishing Co., 1974), 66–67.

2. Caesarius, *Sermo* 52,5.

3. We are indebted to our friend Larry Samuels, M.D., author of *Cancer Diagnosis in Children* (Cleveland: C.R.C. Press, 1972), for not only teaching us the importance of prayer for guidance, but also for helping us understand the relationship between emotions and illnesses such as cancer.

4. Hans Kung, *On Being a Christian* (Garden City, N.Y.: Doubleday, 1976), 577.

5. Further information can be obtained by writing: Assn. of Christian Therapists, St. Vincent Hospital & Medical Center, 2213 Cherry St., Toledo, Ohio 43608

Chapter 9

1. *Rite of Anointing,* 15.

Chapter 11

1. Placid Murray, O.S.B., "The Liturgical History of Extreme Unction," *The Furrow,* XI (1960), 578.

2. Eligius, *De rectitudine catholicae conversationis,* 5.

3. James Brassil, *And I Will Fill This House With Glory: Renewal Within a Suburban Parish* (Locust Valley, N.Y.: Living Flame Press, 1977).

4. Agnes Sanford, *The Healing Light* (Plainfield, N.J.: Logos, 1947).

Chapter 12

1. Boone Porter, "The Origin of the Medieval Rite for Anointing the Sick or Dying," *The Journal of Theological Studies* New Series 7:2 (October, 1956), 214-223.

2. *Rite of Anointing,* 16.

HEALING CASSETTE TAPES

by

Barbara Shlemon, Matt and Dennis Linn

Workshop-Retreat on Healing the Whole Person
(4 tapes)

.... 1. Ministering to Burnt-Out Ministers'
Emotions: Good or Bad?

.... 2. Power in Inner Healing

.... 3. Developing Our Healing Gifts

.... 4. Sacrament of Anointing

—Feel free to make copies of tapes for friends. Individual tapes $3.00 each. Set of 4 tapes $10.

Please send payment along with your order to:

ALU, INC.
504 Antioch
Ballwin, Missouri 63011

Include your

NAME _____

ADDRESS _____

CITY _____ STATE _____ ZIP _____